Let's Talk About Love

A Journey to the End of Taste

Carl Wilson

continuum

NEW YORK • LONDON

2010

The Continuum International Publishing Group Inc
80 Maiden Lane, New York, NY 10038

The Continuum International Publishing Group Ltd
The Tower Building, 11 York Road, London SE1 7NX

www.continuumbooks.com
33third.blogspot.com

Library of Congress Cataloging-in-Publication Data

Wilson, Carl, 1967-
Let's talk about love : a journey to the end of taste / Carl Wilson.
p. cm. -- (33 1/3)
ISBN-13: 978-0-8264-2788-5 (pbk. : alk. paper)
ISBN-10: 0-8264-2788-X (pbk. : alk. paper) 1. Dion, Céline--Criticism
and interpretation. 2. Popular music--History and criticism. 3. Dion,
Céline. Let's talk about love. I. Title. II. Series.
ML420.D565W55 2007
782.42164092--dc22

2007040095

Contents

1.
Let's Talk About Hate

"Hell is other people's music," wrote the cult musician Momus in a 2006 column for *Wired* magazine. He was talking about the intrusive soundtracks that blare in malls and restaurants, but his rewrite of Jean-Paul Sartre conveys a familiar truth: When you hate a song, the reaction tends to come in spasms. Hearing it can be like having a cockroach crawl up your sleeve: you can't flick it away fast enough. But why? And why, in fact, do each of us hate some songs, or the entire output of some musicians, that millions upon millions of other people adore?

In the case of me and Céline Dion, it was Madonna's smirk at the 1998 Oscars that sealed it. That night in March, the galleries of Los Angeles's Shrine Auditorium were the colosseum for the latest gladiatorial contest in which art's frail emissaries would get flattened by the thundering chariots of mass culture. And Empress Madonna would laugh.

Until that evening, I'd done as well as anyone could to keep from colliding with *Titanic*, the all-media juggernaut that had been cutting full-steam through theaters, celebrity rags and radio playlists since Christmas. I hadn't seen the movie and didn't own a TV, but the magazines and websites I read reinforced my sureness that the blockbuster was a pandering fabrication, an action chick-flick, perfectly focus-grouped to be foisted on the dating public.

Now, I realize this attitude, and several to follow, probably makes me sound like a total asshole if, like millions of people, you happen to be a fan of *Titanic* or of the woman who sang its theme. You may be right. Much of this book is about reasonable people carting around cultural assumptions that make them assholes to millions of strangers. But bear with me. At the time, I thought I had plenty of backup.

For instance, Suck.com, that late 90s fount of whip-smart online snark, called *Titanic* a "14-hour-long piece of cinematic vaudeville" that "had the most important thing a movie can have: a clear plot that teaches us important new stuff like if you're incredibly good-looking you'll fall in love." It was contrasted with Harmony Korine's *Gummo*, a film about malformed but somehow radiant teenagers drifting around rural, tornado-devastated Xenia, Ohio—as if, after the twister, Dorothy's Kansas had been transformed into its own eschatological Oz. Suck said that *Gummo* evoked "the vertigo we encounter when people discover and make up new standards of cool and beauty," a sensation resisted by mass society because those standards could be "the wrong ones, and we can't allow ourselves to look at that too hard or long."

CNN.com's review, on the other hand, described *Gummo* as "the cinematic equivalent of Korine making fart noises, folding his eyelids inside-out, and eating boogers," and the director as a punk-ass straining in vain to be a punk.

For cred, the writer namechecked the Sex Pistols, saying that unlike theirs, Korine's rebellion came down to making fun of the hicks.

I knew which argument I bought, and it wasn't just because the same CNN reviewer called *Titanic* "one swell ride." After all, Korine was a lyrical *enfant terrible* who'd gotten fan letters from Werner Herzog; *Titanic* director James Cameron made Sylvester Stallone flicks. Korine was New York and Cameron was Hollywood. And just consider their soundtracks: *Gummo* had a soundscape of doom-metal bands, with an alleviating dash of gospel and Bach. *Titanic* had Celtic pennywhistles, saccharine strings and . . . Céline Dion.

Living in Montreal, Quebec, made it impossible to elude *Titanic*'s musical attack as neatly as the celluloid one. Dion had been intimate with the whole province for years, as first a child star, then a diva of all French-speaking nations and finally an English–French crossover smash. Her rendition of James Horner and Will Jennings's "My Heart Will Go On" had come out first on her bestselling 1997 album *Let's Talk About Love*, then on the bestselling movie soundtrack and then again on a bestselling single. (Ten years later, by some measures, it's the fourteenth-most-successful pop song the world has ever seen.) I hadn't listened regularly to pop radio since I was eleven, and I got agoraphobic in malls, but that tin-flute intro would tootle at me from wall speakers in cafés, falafel joints and corner stores, and in taxis when I could afford them. Dodging "My Heart Will Go On" in 1997–98 would have required a Unabomber-like retreat from audible civilization.

What's more, I was a music critic. I hadn't been one long: I'd done arts writing at a student paper, veered into leftish political journalism and then become the arts editor at one of Montreal's downtown "alternative weeklies." I wrote profiles and CD reviews on the side for the rakish punk-rock guitarist who edited the music section (when he dragged himself into the office in the mid-afternoon). I championed experimentalists and the kinds of unpopular-song writers I was prone to calling "literate." I would not have deigned to listen to an entire Céline Dion album, but it was a basic cultural competency in Montreal to know her hits well enough to mock them with precision. In Quebec, Dion was a cultural fact you could bear with grudging amusement—a horror show, but *our* horror show—until *Titanic* overturned all proportion and Dion's ululating tonsils dilated to swallow the world.

* * *

With "My Heart Will Go On," Céline-bashing became not just a Canadian hobby but a nearly universal pastime. Then-*Village Voice* music editor Robert Christgau described her popularity as a trial to be endured. Rob Sheffield of *Rolling Stone* called her voice "just furniture polish." As late as 2005, her megahit would be ranked the No. 3 "Most Annoying Song Ever" in *Maxim* magazine: "The second most tragic event ever to result from that fabled ocean liner continues to torment humanity years later, as Canada's cruelest shows off a voice as loud as a sonic boom, though not nearly so pretty." A 2006 BBC TV special went two better and named "My Heart Will Go On" the No. 1 most irritating song, and in 2007 England's *Q* magazine elected Dion one of the three worst pop singers of all time, accusing her of "grinding out every note as if bearing some kind of grudge against the very notion of economy."

The black belt in invective has to go to Cintra Wilson, whose anti–celebrity-culture book *A Massive Swelling* describes Dion as "the most wholly repellant woman ever to sing songs of love," singling out "the eye-bleeding *Titanic* ballad" as well as her "unctuous mewling with Blind Italian Opera Guys in loud emotional primary coloring." Wilson concluded: "I think most people would rather be processed through the digestive tract of an anaconda than be Céline Dion for a day."

My personal favorite is the episode of *Buffy the Vampire Slayer* in which Buffy moves into her freshman university dorm and her roommate turns out to be, literally, a demon— the first clue being that she tacks a Céline Dion poster up on their wall. But the catalogue of slams, from critics to Sunday columnists and talk-show hosts to *Saturday Night Live*, could fill this book. I've mostly seconded those emotions, even when a blog ran a Dion joke contest that produced the riddle, "Q: Why did they take the Céline Dion inflatable sex doll off the market? A: It sucked too hard."

But it was at the Oscars that things got personal.

* * *

The night was the expected *Titanic* sweep, capped by director James Cameron's bellowing self-quotation, "I'm the king of the world!" (Which from that podium sounded like, "My brand has total multiplatform synergy!") But in the Best Original Song category, *Titanic*—and Dion—had one unlikely rival, and it happened to be Elliott Smith.

Smith was a hero of mine and of the late-90s indie subculture, one of those "literate," bedroom-recording songwriters whose take on cool and beauty seemed leagues away from the pop-glamour machine. Pockmarked and shy, with a backstory that included childhood abuse and (though I didn't know it yet) on-and-off heroin addiction, he had recorded mainly for the tiny northwestern Kill Rock Stars label, but had just signed to Dreamworks, which would release his next album, *XO*, that summer.

Smith wrote songs whose sighing melodies served as bait for lyrics laced with corrosive rage. They dangled glimpses of a sun "raining its guiding light down on everyone," but everyone in them got burned. They were catchy like a fish hook. As his biographer Benjamin Nugent later wrote in *Elliott Smith and the Ballad of Big Nothing*, "Smith effectively deploys substance abuse as a metaphor for other forms of self-destructive behavior, and the metaphor is a handy one for several reasons. For one, a songwriter taking substance abuse as his literal subject (even if love is the figurative one) can easily steer clear of the Céline Dion clichés of contemporary Top 40 music, the language of hearts, embraces, great divides. [Instead] he participates in a hipper tradition, that of Hank Williams, Johnny Cash and Kurt Cobain—their addiction laments, disavowals and caustic self-portraits."

Smith also dealt frankly, I felt, with one of the ruling paradoxes for partisans of "alternative" culture: It might look like you were asserting superiority over the multitudes, but as a former bullied kid, I always figured it started from rejection. If respect or simple fairness were denied you, you'd build a great life (the best revenge) from what you could scrounge outside their orbit, freed from the thirst for majority approbation. This dynamic is frequently rehearsed in Smith's songs: In "2:45 a.m.," a night prowl that begins by "looking for the man who attacked me / while everybody was laughing at me" ends with "walking out on Center Circle / Been pushed away and I'll never come back." If laments and disavowals were your lot, you would shine those turds until they gleamed. And you'd spread the word to the rest of the alienated, walking wounded—which, in a late-capitalist consumer society, I thought, ought to include everyone but the rich—that they too could find sustenance and sympathy in a voluntary exile.

So how had Smith ended up in center circle at the Shrine Auditorium, smack up against the "Céline Dion clichés," a juxtaposition that seemed as improbable as *Gummo* winning Best Picture? An accident, really. Years before, he'd met independent filmmaker Gus Van Sant hanging out in the Portland bars where Smith's first band, Heatmiser, played. That friendship led to writing songs for Van Sant's first "major motion picture," *Good Will Hunting*, and so to Oscar night, featuring (as *Rolling Stone* put it) "one of the strangest billings since Jimi Hendrix opened for the Monkees," with Smith alongside the pap trio of Trisha Yearwood, Michael Bolton and Céline Dion.

He tried to refuse the invitation, "but then they said that if I didn't play it, they would get someone else to play the song," he told *Under the Radar* magazine. "They'd get someone like Richard Marx to do it. I think when they said that, they had done their homework on me a little bit. Or maybe Richard Marx is a universal scare tactic."

(Richard Marx, for those who've justifiably forgotten, was the balladeer who in 1989 sang, "Wherever you go, whatever you do, I will be right here waiting for you"—threatening enough? But if Dion hadn't been booked, her name might have worked too.)

On Oscar night, Madonna introduced the performers.

Smith ended up following Trisha Yearwood's rendition of *Con Air*'s "How Do I Live?" (written by Dianne Warren, who also penned "Because You Loved Me" and "Love Can Move Mountains" for Dion). He shuffled onstage in a bright white suit loaned by Prada—all he wore of his own was his underwear—and sang "Miss Misery," *Good Will Hunting*'s closing love song to depression. The Oscar producers had refused to let Smith sit on a stool, leaving him stranded clutching his guitar on the wide bare stage. The song seemed as small and gorgeous as a sixteenth-century Persian miniature.

And what came next? Céline Dion swooshing out in clouds of fake fog, dressed in an hourglass black gown, on a set where a white-tailed orchestra was arrayed to look like they were on the deck of the *Titanic* itself. She'd played the Oscars several times, and brought on her full range of gesticulations and grimaces, at one point pounding her chest so robustly it nearly broke the chain on her multimillion-dollar replica of the movie's "Heart of the Ocean" diamond necklace. Then Dion, Smith and Yearwood joined hands and bowed in what *Rolling Stone* called a "bizarre Oscar sandwich."

"It got personal," Smith said later, "with people saying how fragile I looked on stage in a white suit. There was just all of this focus, and people were saying all this stuff simply because I didn't come out and command the stage like Céline Dion does."

And when Madonna opened the envelope to reveal that the Oscar went to "My Heart Would Go On," she snorted and said, "What a shocker."

I liked Madonna, who danced on the art/commerce borderline as nimbly as anyone. But right then, I squeezed my fists wishing she'd preserved a more dignified neutrality ("dignified neutrality" being the phrase that springs right to mind when you say "Madonna"). In retrospect, I realize she was making fun of the predictability, not of Elliott Smith; my umbrage only showed how overinvested I was. I wasn't surprised the Oscars had behaved like the Oscars, that the impossibly good-looking people had spotted each other across the room and as usual run sighing into one another's arms. But the carnivalesque reversal that wedged Elliott in there with Céline and Trisha was one of those rips in the cultural-space continuum that make you feel anything may happen. I was enough of a populist even then to dream that love might move mountains and heal the great divide.

But when Madonna seemed to chuckle at Elliott Smith, the grudge was back on. And not with Madonna. With Céline Dion.

* * *

Lamentably, this story requires a coda: Elliott Smith had an adverse reaction to his dose of fame. Paranoid that his friends resented him, he distanced himself, relapsing into mood swings and substance abuse, even public brawls. His songwriting suffered, with the so-so *Figure 8* in 2000 and then zip until 2003, when he reportedly had sobered up and was finishing a new album. Then, on October 21, 2003, police in Los Angeles got a call from Smith's girlfriend in their Echo Park apartment. They had been arguing. She had locked herself in the bathroom. Then she heard a scream. She came out to find Smith with a steak knife plunged into his chest, dead at thirty-four.

I hadn't thought much about the Oscar debacle between 1998 and 2003. I'd moved from Montreal to Toronto, from the alternative weekly to a large daily paper, gotten married (to a woman with a severe *Gummo* fixation), and settled into a new circle of friends. But the day Smith died, I flashed back to that night when the whole world had gotten to hear what one of its fragile, unlovely outcasts had to offer, and it answered, *No, we'd prefer Céline Dion.*

"Tastes," wrote the poet Paul Valéry, "are composed of a thousand distastes." So when the idea came to me recently to examine the mystery of taste—of what keeps *Titanic* people and *Gummo* people apart—by looking closely at a very popular artist I really, really can't stand, Dion was waiting at the front of the line.

2.
Let's Talk About Pop
(and Its Critics)

I did not hate Céline Dion solely on Elliott Smith's account. From the start, her music struck me as bland monotony raised to a pitch of obnoxious bombast—R&B with the sex and slyness surgically removed, French *chanson* severed from its wit and soul—and her repertoire as Oprah Winfrey–approved chicken soup for the consumerist soul, a neverending crescendo of personal affirmation deaf to social conflict and context. In celebrity terms, she was another dull Canadian goody-goody. She could barely muster up a decent personal scandal, aside from the pre-existing squick-out of her marriage to the twice-her-age Svengali who began managing her when she was twelve.

As far as I knew, I had never even *met* anybody who liked Céline Dion.

My disdain persisted after I left the Céline ground zero of Montreal, and even as my enchantment with "underground" cultural commandments weakened and my feelings warmed to more mainstream music. I can't claim any originality in that shift. I went through it in synch with the entire field of music criticism, save the most ornery holdouts and hotheaded kids. It came with startling speed. A new generation moved into positions of critical influence, and many of them cared more about hip-hop or electronica or Latin music than about rock, mainstream or otherwise. They mounted a wholesale critique against the syndrome of measuring all popular music by the norms of rock culture—"rockism," often set against "pop-ism" or "poptimism." Online music blogs and discussion forums sped up the circulation of such trends of opinion. The Internet pushed aside intensive album listening in favor of a download-and-graze mode that gives pop novelty more chance to shine. And downloading also broke the corporate record companies' near-monopoly over music distribution, which made taking up arms against the mass-culture music Leviathan seem practically redundant.

Plus, some fantastic pop happened to be coming out, and everyone wanted to talk about it. In a Toronto bookstore in 1999, a bright young experimental guitarist caught me off guard by asking if I had heard the teen diva Aaliyah's hit, "Are You That Somebody." I hadn't, but I soon would. That rhythmically topsy-turvy R&B track was produced by Timothy Mosley, a.k.a. Timbaland, and he and his peers began making the pop charts a freshly polymorphous playground. *Après Timbaland, la deluge:* critics started noticing a kindred creativity even in despised teen pop, and by 2007, writers at prestige publications like *The New York Times* and the haughty old *New Yorker* could be found praising one-hit R&B wonders and "mall punk" teen bands as much as Bruce Springsteen or U2.

This was the outcome of many cycles of revisionism: one way a critic often can get noticed is by arguing that some music everyone has trashed is in fact genius, and over the years that process has "reclaimed" genres from metal to disco to lounge exotica and prog rock, and artists from ABBA to Motorhead. *Rolling Stone*'s jeers notwithstanding, the Monkees are now as critically respectable as Jimi Hendrix. Even antebellum blackface minstrel music has been reassessed, its melodies as well as its racial pathologies found to lie at the twisted root of American popular song.

This epidemic of second thought made critical scorn generally seem a tad shady: If critics were so wrong about disco in the 1970s, why not about Britney Spears now? Why did pop music have to get old before getting a fair shake? Why did it have to be a "guilty" pleasure? Once pop criticism had a track record lengthy enough to be full of wrong turns, neither popular nor critical consensus seemed like a reliable guide. Why not just follow your own enjoyment? Unless you have a thing for white-power anthems, the claim now goes, there is no reason ever to feel guilty or ashamed about what you like. And I agree, though it's curious how often critics' "own enjoyment" still takes us all down similar paths at once.

The collective realignment was also a market correction. After the tumult of the early 1990s, when "underground" music was seized on by the mainstream and just as quickly thrown overboard, many critics and "underground" fans got in a cynical mood. The ever-present gap between critical and general tastes threatened to become an entrenched war of position, in which liking "critics' darlings" like Elliott Smith and liking pop stars became mutually exclusive. It wasn't sustainable. An academic might be able to dismiss public taste completely in favor of the weird and challenging, but a working pop critic who did so would be (rightly) out of a job in the long run. And the "underground" thing was becoming a rut of its own.

However attenuated, though, the gap between critical acclaim and popular success never goes away. It's visible every December when critics draw up best-of-the-year lists on which Radiohead, Ghostface or Bob Dylan eclipse most of the chart-toppers (though no longer all of them). On movie critics' lists, too, summer blockbusters take a back seat to comparative box-office dwarfs: intense domestic dramas, "indie" black comedies, Henry James adaptations. This split is so routine it has come to seem organic. People often say it's just a matter of aesthetic education and exposure to greater volumes of material, but that seems to imply critical judgments are more objective and lasting, when the record shows us they're not.

In the end, if delight is where you find it and myriad pop pleasures meet the heterodox needs of diverse publics, what is the real substance of the dislike I and so many other commentators have for Céline Dion?

Yet Dion remains, as the British critic and sociologist Simon Frith remarked in a 2002 interview with the website rockcritics.com, "probably the most loathed superstar I can remember, at least by everyone I know, not just critics but even my mother-in-law." He added, "I doubt if she will ever be redeemed, ABBA-style, and what seems to concern everyone is that she is just naff."

And Frith is a Dion *fan*.

* * *

Back when heavy metal got no respect (i.e., five years ago), Deena Weinstein wrote an essay in its defense called "Rock

Critics Need Bad Music," which pointed out that critical authority depends on the power to exclude, not just to canonize. It hinges on turning your readership into an in-crowd, smarter than some less-discerning audience. Then, when a genre like metal or a band like ABBA is resuscitated, everyone pretends they were never one of the people who looked down on it. The easy conclusion would be that critics' tastes are opportunistic. But this fungibility is part of taste's standard wiring.

Everyone has a taste biography, a narrative of shifting preferences: I remember at age twelve telling people I liked "all kinds of music, *except* disco and country," two genres I now adore. My hometown was a very white, Ontario-rustbelt city in bad decline. I was a middle-class bookworm who started with the Beatles from my parents' record collection but soon hit the harder stuff, setting out on the great expedition of the avant-garde. It was only after I moved away that I began to grasp that my blind spots were a regional and cultural bias. My tastes were reshaped by social experiences: dancing in Montreal gay clubs where body-rocking techno mixed seamlessly into disco classics; making friends from Texas or the country-loving Canadian Maritimes; visiting the US South. They were also altered by musical information—by realizing how many hip-hop samples came from disco, for instance, or by following the links from Bob Dylan to Hank Williams to Johnny Cash and the 60s Nashville Sound, and finally back to contemporary country. I realized my easy scorn had betrayed an ignorance of whole communities and ways of life, prejudices I did not want to live with. The epiphany was ethical, but it led to musical enjoyment. Recent talk about pop taste, about unguilty pleasure, tends to trace the route the other way around, if it even gets to ethics.

At twelve, my dislike of disco and country didn't feel like a social opinion. It felt like a musical reaction. I flinched at the very sound of Dolly Parton or Donna Summer, as unaware that I had any choice about finding them stupid as I was of the frameworks in which they were smart. It seemed natural: I hated disco and country, as cleanly and purely as I now hate Céline Dion.

So how cleanly and purely is that? After all, as I'm writing this, Dion has sold 175 million albums, not counting the *Titanic* soundtrack. She has five recordings in the Recording Industry Association of America's list of the Top 100 albums by sales, making her the twenty-third-bestselling pop act of all time. Globally she is the most successful French-language singer ever and could be the bestselling female singer. For four years her legions have tithed their salaries to fly to Las Vegas for her nightly revue *A New Day* in the custom-built Colosseum theater at Caesar's Palace. She is beloved by people from Idaho to Iraq, who trade news and debate favorites on Internet message boards like any other group of fans. They cook, work out and date to her music, and when weightier events come, her songs are there, for first dances at weddings and processions at funerals.

When the singer herself is asked if her critics bother her, she answers as she did to *Elle* magazine in a 2007 interview: "We've been sold out for four years. *The audience is my answer.*"

Which doesn't mean you have to admire her. Unless maybe it does. Certainly a critical generation determined to swear off elitist bias does seem called to account for the immense international popularity of someone we've designated so devoid of appeal. Those who find Dion "naff"—British for tacky, gauche, kitschy or, as they say in Quebec, *kétaine*—must be overlooking something, maybe beginning with why we have labels like tacky and naff. If guilty pleasures are out of date, perhaps the time has come to conceive of a *guilty displeasure*. This is not like the nagging regret I have about, say, never learning to like opera. My aversion to Dion more closely resembles how put off I feel when someone says they're pro-life or a Republican: intellectually I'm aware how personal and complicated such affiliations can be, but my gut reactions are more crudely tribal.

Musical subcultures exist because our guts tell us certain kinds of music are for certain kinds of people. The codes are not always transparent. We are attracted to a song's beat, its edge, its warmth, its idiosyncrasy, the singer's *je ne sais quoi*; we check out the music our friends or cultural guides commend. But it's hard not to notice how those processes reflect and contribute to self-definition, how often persona and musical taste happen to jibe. It's most blatant in the identity war that is high school, but music never stops being a badge of recognition. And in the offhand rhetoric of dismissal—"teenybopper pap," "only hippies like that band," "sounds like music for date rapists"—we bar the doors of the clubs we don't want to claim us as members. Psychoanalysis would say our aversions can tell us more than our conscious desires about what we are, unwillingly, drawn to. What unpleasant truths might we learn from looking closer at our musical fears and loathings, at what we consider "bad taste"?

The Céline Dion fan-club roster that many non-fans picture was outed with bracingly open elitism by the *Independent on Sunday* in the UK in 1999, in the paper's "Why are they famous?" series: "Wedged between vomit and indifference, there must be a fan base: some middle-of-the-road Middle England invisible to the rest of us. Grannies, tux-wearers, overweight children, mobile-phone salesmen and shopping-centre devotees, presumably."

Reading that, my heart swells for these maligned wearers of inappropriate tuxedos, these poignantly tubby prepubescents pining away to the strains of songs of love sung by a pretty lady with the best voice in the whole world. And far more than I hate Céline Dion, I hate this anonymous staffer from the *Independent on Sunday*. But he's only fleshing out the implication in, for instance, my use of the phrase "Oprah Winfrey-approved." If his portrayal of Dion's audience is accurate, it includes mostly people who, aboard the *Titanic*, would have perished in steerage. If my disdain for her extends to them, am I trying to deny them a lifeboat?

The *Independent*'s bile demonstrates why the critical redemption of abject music tends to come years after its heyday: lounge exotica stops sounding like a pathetic seduction soundtrack on the hi-fi of a smarmy insurance salesman and starts to sound charmingly strange, governed by a lost and thus beguiling musical rulebook. In the present tense, submerged social antagonisms and the risk of being taken for one of the "tacky" dullards make it less attractive to be so all-embracing—to hear Céline Dion as history might hear her.

* * *

This book is an experiment in taste, in stepping deliberately outside one's own aesthetics. It has to do with social affinities and rancors and what art and its appreciation can do to mediate or exacerbate them. At a time when the whole issue of the meaning and purpose of art has grown very murky, the exercise might open a few windows. Primarily, though, the question is whether anyone's tastes stand on solid ground, starting with mine.

One condition, I think, is that the dislike in question has some personal bite. A random target won't do. While I generally give a wide berth to any epic pop ballad, the fact that Céline Dion is a Canadian makes her more grating than Michael Bolton: shots at her come with collateral damage to my entire country, as in the *South Park* movie anthem, "Blame Canada," which crows, "When Canada is dead and gone / There'll be no more Céline Dion." I feel implicated: "Hold on," I want to protest, "we hated her before you did!"

My test case will be *Let's Talk About Love*, the album that includes "My Heart Will Go On." It's not her bestselling release (that would be 1996's *Falling Into You*), nor the most esteemed among her fans. But it was huge, and came out at the peak of both Dion's fame and my animosity. Besides, what better title for a study of cultural passions and antipathies?

Along with immersing myself in this record, I'll examine Dion the same way I do any artist I get interested in—her background, career and influences, the genre she belongs to, what sensibility she expresses. But I'll also look at taste itself, what has been said about it, its role in aesthetic theory and the research that's been done scientifically and not-so-scientifically. Will I find my inner Céline Dion fan? The goal isn't to end in a group hug. If I end up warming to her music, that will be one lesson; if I don't, we might draw others.

As a goodwill gesture, let's proceed on a first-name basis, the way her fans do: Hi there, Céline.

The exercise isn't as far as it seems from my usual critical leanings, toward knotty music like art rock, psych-folk, post-punk, free jazz or the more abstract ends of techno and hip-hop. I write about such sounds in the belief that "difficult" music can help shake up perceptions, push us past habitual limits. As Simon Frith wrote in his book *Performing Rites,* difficult listening bears in it the traces of a "utopian impulse, the negation of everyday life"—an opening toward "another world in which [the difficult] would be 'easy.'" And isn't Céline Dion, for me, actually more "difficult" music than any postmodern noise collage? It sure is more uncomfortable. It could turn out to be more disorienting than the kinds of "difficulty" I've come to take for granted.

Whatever Céline's merits, after all, they are not sonic innovation, verbal inventiveness, social criticism, rough exuberance, erotic charge or any of the other qualities I and a lot of critics listen for. Her fans must hear something else. What is it, and in what language might it be addressed? Hard as it is to admit, part of the answer could lie in the music's very mundanity. After years of pursuing music in which the "difficulty" carries intimations of "another world," sonic forecasts of transformation, I've begun to wonder whether "easier" music might contain hints for reconciliation with the world into which we're already thrown. Maybe it deals with problems that don't require leaps of imagination but require other efforts, like patience, or compromise. There may be negations there, but not the ones I'm used to.

At the same time compromise is what worries me: Maybe I am heading down a relativistic rabbit hole. If even Céline can be redeemed, is there no good or bad taste, or good and bad art? If I decided not to condemn the sleek musical baubles of Céline Dion, would I also have to reconsider the facile decorations of glass sculptor Dale Chihuly, or the kitsch paintings of Thomas Kinkade, "Painter of Light™"? Kinkade is the most commercially successful painter of our time, whose nostalgically purified landscapes, untouched by trouble, humor or irony, command hundreds of thousands of dollars from followers outside the art scene. What about mediocre books, or the doublespeak of conservative punditry? Maybe if you don't stand for something you'll fall for anything.

Maybe if hating Céline Dion is wrong, I don't want to be right.

Whatever the perils, it turns out I have an unexpected ally.

* * *

In refreshing my memory about the 1998 Oscars, I came across a story I had never heard: Elliott Smith admitted to the music zine *Comes with a Smile* that he arrived that night "prepared to keep a lot of distance from Céline Dion. I thought she'd blow in with her bodyguards and be a weird superstar to everybody," he said. "But she wasn't like that at all."

"She was really sweet," he added in another interview, "which has made it impossible for me to dislike Céline Dion anymore. Even though I can't stand the music that she makes—with all due respect, I don't like it much at all—she herself was very, very nice. She asked me if I was nervous and I said, 'Yeah.' And she was like, 'That's good, because you get your adrenaline going, and it'll make your song better. It's a beautiful song.' Then she gave me a big hug. It was too much. It was too human to be dismissed simply because I find her music trite."

Smith's friend Marc Swanson, a visual artist, gave biographer Nugent this account of what came next: "[After] this, we'd constantly be running into people coming up and talking to him, people who didn't know him, and saying, 'Oh, how's it goin', saw you on the Oscars, so how was that?' And [they'd] make some derogatory Céline Dion comment, and every time they'd do it, I'd be like, 'gasp,' and this look of rage in his eyes would come up and he'd be like, 'You know, she's a really nice person.' And they'd always recoil and be like, 'Oh, no, I'm sure she's really nice.' . . . I thought that was a cute thing about him: He was defending Céline Dion all the time."

And Smith only met Céline once. Just think, if we lingered longer, maybe we'd find something "too human to be dismissed" even in her music.

3.
Let's Talk in French

Eight of the oddest, most widely mocked minutes of Céline Dion's career come September 3, 2005, on a Larry King TV special about the wreck of the Gulf Coast by Hurricane Katrina. In the interview, Céline waves her arms, shouts and weeps, blubberingly decries the war in Iraq and cheers on roving gangs of looters in New Orleans. Then she takes a deep breath and croons a pop aria to God.

Online video clips the next day run under headlines like, "Celine Dion goes crazy!" But actually it may be the best glimpse of the "real" Céline most of the world ever gets. To see why, we have to go through the looking glass, into her home province of Quebec.

* * *

Each June 24, Quebec celebrates its version of Independence Day. It has parades, cookouts, fireworks and flags. All it lacks is the independence.

CARL WILSON

Saint Jean-Baptiste Day, the Catholic solstice feast, was secularized by the province in 1977 as La Fête National du Québec, the "national" holiday. Every year I was in Montreal, my mostly anglophone (English-speaking) friends and I would head down to the parade and marvel at how little most of us understood about the culture in which we lived, like expatriates in our own country. Under an invariably bright blue sky, women with big hair and men with bigger hair would stand up in convertibles to blow kisses to a roaring throng. And in nine out of ten cases, my friends—who had come as students at Montreal's two English universities and then stayed, boots stuck in the sweet molasses of the city's sybaritic lifestyle—had little clue who these objects of adulation were. "I'm pretty sure that guy's a talk-show host," Susana might hazard. "And she's gotta be an actress, right?" "No," Gordon might put in. "She's the books columnist for *Le Devoir.*" There were movie stars and weather presenters, restaurateurs and circus performers, each hailed like a Beatle landing at Kennedy airport, if the Beatles also happened to be your second cousins.

This is Quebec's *vedette* (star) culture, a Bizarro Hollywood's worth of celebrities who exist to hardly anyone but the six million francophone (French-speaking) Quebec citizens to whom they are favorite siblings of a nation in perpetual waiting. And it is from *vedette* ranks that Céline Dion was chosen as princess and guardian angel or, as the press there say, "our national Céline." To most of the world, Céline is a North American pop singer and maybe secondly a Canadian who speaks French. At home she is a *Québécoise* first and forever, and the implications permeate her career, including why nonfans stare at her triumphs with the same bewilderment I felt watching the super-unknown stars march by at the foot of rue Saint-Denis.

Vedette mania's strangeness to outsiders—always fashionably dressed, seldom remotely hip—is an inspired cultural answer to a political problem, safeguarding Quebec's character as one of the world's most privileged postcolonial societies, like Scotland if it still spoke Gaelic but were as well-off as the Swiss. For much of the twentieth century, francophones felt like unwanted guests in the province where they held a majority. Their centuries-old conquest still stung, because the English business class—in collusion with the Canadian government and a repressive French Catholic church—retained a lock on money and power. Unilingual French speakers were shut out of better jobs, and if French education weren't protected by the constitution, the language might have faded from use as it did in Louisiana and in most other French pockets of Canada. But the 1960s brought the "Quiet Revolution," a series of upheavals to throw off church moralism and English hegemony. There was even the Front de Libération du Québec (FLQ), who committed bombings and ultimately a political assassination that drove Canada's grooviest-ever prime minister, Pierre Trudeau, quite ungroovily to declare quasi-martial law when Céline was a toddler. FLQ leader Pierre Vallières had written a Franz Fanon–style manifesto titled *Nègres Blancs d'Amérique*—"White Niggers of America." While the population overwhelmingly rejected the FLQ's violent self-appointment as Quebec's Black Panthers, many felt Vallières's analogy was only a mild exaggeration.

The legacy of that era is a nationalist consensus that vacillates between cosmopolitan social democracy and a harder insularity. It led to two failed referenda on separation from

Canada in 1980 and 1995. (The separatist party is in government as I write.) But one reason it's never again leaned toward violence is that the revolution wasn't really quiet: it was secured by an outspoken cultural wing, with music leading the way.

Quebec pop before the 60s meant variety acts, heirs of Montreal's Prohibition-free, roaring-20s vaudeville heyday. They mainly sang translations of foreign hits. The mid-60s brought the *Yé-Yé* craze of French covers of British Invasion rock—the future Mr. Céline, René Angélil, dropped out of high school as a minor star with Beatles knockoffs Les Baronets. But by decade's end the province was peppered with *boîtes à chanson,* clubs where troubadours sang poetry laced with liberation slogans and winter-landscape allegories. By the 70s these *chansonniers* were stars, homegrown Gainsbourgs and Dylans (it was mostly guys). Quebec *chanson* was nationalism's soundtrack. Gilles Vigneault's "Gens du pays" is so well-loved that in Montreal you sing it instead of "Happy Birthday." It's a better singalong, too: *"Gens du pays / C'est à votre tour / De vous laisser parler d'amour."* "People of [this] country, it's your turn to let yourselves talk about love." (Can it be accidental when a later Quebec singer titles an album *Let's Talk About Love*?)

Quebeckers are also among the world's most prolific record buyers, so international record labels became eager to sign the *chansonniers*. But this created division in the local music industry, as enthusiasm never vanished in working-class and rural Quebec for the older-style "variety-pop" interpreters (mostly women) who would inspire the young Céline Dion. Université de Montréal communications professor Line Grenier, a scholar of Quebec pop and especially "the Céline phenomenon," illuminated the situation for me: "The milieu was really split in two between the *chanson*—intellectual, leftist-oriented—and the variety-pop. There were two totally different networks, two different sets of record labels, different kinds of career management."

This brought the sort of pigeonholing, of merely "commercial" singers versus "deeper" performers, that we know from everyday music talk. But the consequences were the opposite of most pop markets: The artistic *chansonniers* not only got the good reviews, citations in political speeches and spotlights at Fête National concerts; they also got big corporate deals. Most variety interpreters recorded for smaller local labels, and not only critics but music-business bigwigs deplored them as throwbacks, as *kétaine*, meaning not only tacky but hickish. When in 1979 the industry launched its own Grammys, the Félix awards (after *chanson* pioneer Félix Leclerc), it had to add a "people's choice" slot or no variety singer could have won a prize.

But the 1980 referendum shook up everything. Separation was defeated narrowly enough to knock out investor confidence in the midst of an international recession. Quebec's economy would not fully recover for two decades. Multinational labels pulled back, dropping everyone but major stars. To pick up the slack, local variety-pop labels were joined by companies created with government funding, and music became a made-in-Quebec business: as Grenier explains, the *chanson* and variety camps, snobs and *kétaines,* still didn't like each other, but had to unite to rebuild. It was into this disoriented industry that Céline made her debut.

* * *

Céline Marie Claudette Dion was born in 1968 in Charle-magne, a unilingual French-Catholic suburb of fewer than six thousand people a half hour northeast of Montreal. Her rags-to-riches story is a paragon of the genre: The youngest of fourteen children for Adhémar Dion and Thérèse Tanguay (later well known as "Maman Dion"), Céline was twenty-two years younger than her oldest sister. The kids slept several to a bed. Adhémar supported them on $165 a week as a butcher and later in a factory job. The one relief was music—they all played instruments—and eventually the Dions saved enough to lease a piano bar, where the kids waited tables and, between shifts, sang. Including, from age five, baby Céline. She lived to perform—"for me, singing was the *real* life, not two plus two equals four"—and when she was twelve, the family helped her make a demo tape of a song cowritten by brother Jacques and Maman Dion. They mailed it to René Angélil, now known as the manager of the 1970s' biggest variety-pop artist, Ginette Reno. After some harassment, he allowed an audition, and at the sound of Céline's pipes, legend has it, he wept and swore to make her a star.

There were no prospects at labels so René, a notorious gambler, mortgaged his house to put her album out. Quebec radio said her syrupy ballads were fit only for nursing homes, but she caught on as a novelty in France, which sent her as its representative to the 1982 Yamaha World Popular Song Festival in Tokyo. She won, and as so often in Canada, foreign praise raised her stock *chez nous*. Soon Céline was selling hundreds of thousands of records in Quebec and touring internationally. The *chanson*-minded elites remained unmoved. When she sang for Pope John Paul II in 1984 at Montreal's Olympic Stadium, it brought back bad memories of Quebec's obeisance to the church. As recalled later by Konrad Yakabuski, Quebec correspondent for the Toronto-based *Globe and Mail* (where I now work), "Ms. Dion, with her double-digit, Roman Catholic family . . . prompted sneers in post–Quiet Revolution cultural circles." Even her future husband admits she was not a cute child: her bushy hair and snaggle teeth led *Croc*, Quebec's *Mad* magazine, to dub her "Canine Dion," the picture of the province's "white trash" underbelly, with louche manager and peasant stage mom at her sides. As pollster Jean-Marc Leger told Yakabuski, "She wasn't simply perceived as *kétaine*—she *was kétaine.*" Years later she would break down in tears on Quebec TV over her early media treatment.

How did she shake off the stigma? By stages. Céline was in a long line of Quebec child stars such as 70s sensations René and Natalie Simard, whose TV variety show was the province's version of Donny and Marie Osmond. But these ingénues seldom achieved adult careers. Angélil realized Céline would have to make a clean break. In an eighteen-month hiatus in the mid-80s, she got her teeth capped, took singing lessons and developed a new repertoire. Her comeback was the breathy 1987 dance-pop single "Lolita," a Madonna-ish number not as suggestive as its title, though it foretold events to come with its theme of a teen girl's crush on an older man. In the video she mooned around in a leather pantsuit with a belt that seemed to be made out of gold records and gazed longingly at ancient castles on hilltops.

Her child-star days were behind her, but it's useful not to forget Céline is that kid who went directly from a gigantic provincial family into a pop finishing school run by the impresario who, like starlets before her, she went on to marry. More than nearly any celebrity short of Michael Jackson, she never had an autonomous phase, never lived in what people call the real world, not even the hothouse variant known as high school. She had other weights to carry on her shoulder pads.

* * *

Céline began to study English as a condition of the deal with CBS (later Sony) that promoted her out of the Quebec label system. The timing was not good: her first English-language album, *Unison*, came out in 1990 as the collapse of the Meech Lake constitutional accord inflamed the rift between Quebec and English Canada. It didn't go unnoticed that she jettisoned the accent from her name on the album cover.

Céline had armloads of Félix awards, but for *Unison* she was nominated as Best Anglophone Artist. In Quebec, those were fighting words, and her response was uncharacteristically pugnacious: she refused the prize on live TV, saying, "I am not an anglophone artist. . . . Everywhere I go in the world, I say I'm proud to be *Québécoise*." Some anglophones were offended but the point was won. Quebec was reassured, and the next year the category was renamed to Quebec Artist Most Illustrious in a Language Other Than French—observers joked you could call it the Céline prize for short. The affair did raise some doubts in the rest of Canada, where her fame was rising with singles like the aptly titled "Where Does My Heart Beat Now?" She calmed that side with another off-message moment, performing in the Canada pavilion at Expo 92 in Spain, where she announced, "I'm against any form of separation, and if there's anything I can do to help, I'll do it." Between the two statements, she neutralized her move into

English and adopted the prototypical Quebecker's stance of favoring, as comedians often put it, an independent Quebec within a united Canada. Her bonafides as a *Québécoise* rarely have been questioned since.

After all, Céline was giving Quebec its first real beachhead in America, where Quebeckers despise the foreign policy but adore Elvis and Mickey Mouse. She and René, like many Quebeckers, became "snowbirds" with a winter place in Florida. They founded a diner chain called Nickels, whose franchises are Googie-style, Naugahyde-interior temples to burgers, bobby sox and 50s rock'n'roll, with a side plate of Céline memorabilia. The peak came in the 1997 Grammys broadcast when she delivered a few words in Quebec *joual* slang, incomprehensible even to most other French speakers. As Yakabuski wrote, "In front of the United States and the world, Ms. Dion proved to Quebeckers that they exist." Then-premier Lucien Bouchard called Céline Quebec's "greatest ambassador." As Grenier puts it, Céline had attained one of her defining roles in Quebec: "national hero."

The next year, the domestic industry finally gave its seal of approval by inviting her to host the 1998 Félix ceremony, alongside childhood idol René Simard and *chansonnier* Jean-Pierre Ferland. The highlight was a comedy sketch in which Céline and impressionist André-Philippe Gagnon imitated the characters Môman (mama) and Pôpa (papa) from the popular series *La petite vie*—one of the weirdest TV hits ever, a working-class family sitcom à la *Roseanne* but more anarchic and grotesque, with actors in stage makeup and false beards, like a live-action *Simpsons*. In the sketch, Gagnon's Pôpa said he wanted to "see big" like René Angélil, and make Môman a star. The press crowed, "Céline as Môman: Who could ask for more?" Grenier argues it was a key moment: the bullying elite was finally able to laugh with Céline, not at her. Quebec's confidence had grown: it was now willing not only to bare its trashy underbelly, but to give it a big, wet kiss. And Céline's casting as Môman was a nod to the contribution of the skinny little hick who had conquered the globe.

But it wasn't all symbolism. She also elevated herself musically.

* * *

If you have never heard Céline Dion in French, it's hard to believe it's the same singer. Her cadences are much more supple and controlled, her interpretations more detailed. Gone is the blank persona that reduces many of her English songs to vocal stunt work, replaced by what can only be called soul.

Could her English material suffer from nothing but a comprehension problem? Not straightforwardly, as her earlier French music is marred by exactly the same much-of-a-muchness. But over the years, her French song selections and arrangements evolved. The effect, perhaps the purpose, was to blur the boundaries that stood between variety-pop and *chanson,* and between Céline and respectability.

Not coincidentally, it began right after she started her English career. Her next French album, in 1991, was devoted to songs by Luc Plamondon, a respected Quebec songwriter renowned in France for his rock musical *Starmania.* Céline's version of one *Starmania* tune became her first No. 1 in years in France, and its subject is far from anything you'd expect: "Un garçon pas comme les autres (Ziggy)" is about a girl's unrequited love for "a boy unlike the others," but ends happily as she resigns herself just to going dancing with him—in gay bars. Céline had given the world its first hit fag-hag ballad. Next, on the hugely successful *D'Eux* (1995) and follow-up *S'il suffisait d'aimer* (1998), she paired with Jean-Jacques Goldman, a *chansonnier* often called France's Bruce Springsteen (not a link many anglo listeners would make with Céline). He is credited with demanding Céline learn to *dechanter*—undersing, not belt to the bleachers—and he brought new colors to her repertoire with country-folk textures and storytelling. Goldman's topics too can be surprising, including a song about AIDS ("*L'amour existe encore*") and one about an Algerian-French immigrant, glad to be free of the veil but lonely for the countrywomen left behind ("*Zora sourit*"). These alliances may have been motivated mainly by Plamondon and Goldman's credibility in France, where post-child-star Céline had gotten a lukewarm hearing. But no doubt Céline and René are also more sensitive to the nuances of their own language, especially since lyrical quality often matters more to French success.

The corollary is that musical quality often seems *less* important, as decades of French-rock jokes will testify. Literary-minded *chanson* aside, French pop markets have lagged behind even when French movies, books and art were at the forefront of innovation. Recent French techno has helped loosen music up considerably, but why Gallic pop is so often so lame is one of those imponderables (is it the linguistic rhythms?) that serve as fodder for Sunday arts section essays.

Which may help explain why it took only minor adjustments for Céline to bridge *chanson* and variety: the gap was exaggerated. It's not that Céline became a legit *chanteuse* (not writing her own songs remains a stroke against her) but the differences stopped mattering so much. She could claim all the institutional trappings that *chanson* monopolized a decade before. Slowly, Grenier says, the term lost its mystique, reverting largely to its generic meaning, just plain "song." That change helped open up Quebec pop. It is now much more eclectic, with more "world music" influence, more bilingualism (even within songs), diverse modes of rock and a growing hip-hop scene. Céline can't take credit—some of these artists would call themselves her nemeses—but she deserves a nod for helping scramble the rulebook.

And the same is true in Quebec culture at large.

* * *

Sneering at Céline in Quebec has never gone wholly out of style. In 1994, there was plenty of backlash to her and René's ridiculously lavish, Princess Diana–style "Royal Wedding" in Montreal. In 2006, people got fed up with wall-to-wall media coverage of the twenty-fifth anniversary of her career, enough that one television newsmagazine aired a special asking if it was possible to criticize Céline and René in public anymore. The hip downtown weekly *Voir* long ago declared it would never cover her and the chief arts critic at highbrow daily *Le Devoir* never tires of deriding a performer he considers the worst of globalized homogeneity with nicknames like "Miss Tupperware."

But as Line Grenier points out, most Quebeckers who detest Céline (including Grenier's own brother-in-law) now append caveats: "Yes, but . . ." But she's been around so long. But she works so hard. But she's been treated so harshly.

"They'd like not to care," Grenier says, "but they can't help it because she's always there. I don't think a week goes by without a mention of Céline in the mainstream media one way or another, and it's not just to talk about her career. It's to talk about all sorts of things. That affects how people react to whether or not she's *kétaine*."

Along with her diplomatic role as national hero, Grenier says, Céline provides Quebec a model of the "happy entrepreneur," not only in her music career and its many spin-offs (fine chocolates, sunglasses, perfumes) but in charitable work (particularly for cystic fibrosis, a disease to which Céline has lost a niece) and, more subtly, her self-discipline (going weeks at a time without speaking in order to protect her vocal cords, for instance). Céline and René's company Les Productions Feeling employs much of her family and scads of other Québécois, a fact far from lost on her compatriots. Indeed, she is one of the province's leading exports, along with the Cirque de Soleil (Céline's partners in her Las Vegas show), and the more avant-garde theater spectacles of director Robert Lepage. These cultural enterprises have cleared a path for "Quebec, Inc.," a new nationalism concerned less with legal sovereignty and more with grounding Quebec's autonomy in an outward-bound dynamism. Today, how Céline sounds matters less than how a Quebec software firm can emulate her global *savoir-faire*. It's quite a turnabout from Quiet Revolution dreams of a socialist "Cuba of the north."

But Céline's ineluctable Quebeckitude remains a block for anglo audiences abroad. When British writer A. A. Gill, in a 2003 anti-Vegas diatribe in *Vanity Fair*, attacked her "ungodly French-Canadian glottal accent," it was remarkable less for its rudeness than for being unusually well informed. To most of the English world, Céline's Frenchness remains a vague thing, almost an affectation; that it represents a whole culture groping its way to self-determination doesn't translate. She is condemned to a kind of pidgin otherness that gains her little in empathy or exotic allure because few know how to place it within standard North American racial and ethnic matrices. If she fails most non-fans' authenticity tests, the trouble may be not only her showbiz upbringing but that her personal touchstones are off the map. Her commercialism does not get the kind of pass given a rapper who fixates on "gettin' paid" or a country singer who thanks God for the hits that rescued her from a Southern shack. Since Quebec is a null set in the popular imagination, Céline is judged by middle-class standards in which "sellout" is always a handy stick to slap down the overreaching.

When Céline talks in the first-person plural—*we* achieved this, *we* hoped for that, *we* decided to make this record—she is speaking of herself, René, her producers, her Charlemagne clan and all of what's called "Team Céline," but symbolically it includes Quebec's extended family. Where she comes from, collectivity counts, and her gains are the gains of a people. It is a recognisable ethic in an African-American star, but in Céline it doesn't read: she represents an opaque referent, rendering her meaning illegible.

* * *

Which brings us back to the Larry King interview. There's no denying its spectacle. From the first, Céline, who had just given a million dollars to the New Orleans relief effort, was in tears. She gasped over explaining the disaster to her son René Charles. She demanded to know why it was hard to send helicopters to rescue New Orleanians from rooftops when "it's so easy to send planes in another country to kill everyone in a second!" The centerpiece was her paean to the joy of looting: "Oh, they're stealing twenty pair of jeans or they're stealing television sets. Who cares? They're not going to go too far with it! . . . Some of the people who do that, they're so poor they've never touched anything in their life. *Let them touch those things for once!*"

Then Larry King, with jawdropping crassness, asked if she had a song for the occasion. Céline did not break into Motorhead's "Eat the Rich." She wiped her eyes and sang "A Prayer," which she'd recorded with blind Italian opera guy Andrea Bocelli, purring piously of "a place where we'll be safe."

"Let them touch those things" instantly joined the annals of unhinged celebrity utterance; the hymn was consigned to plastic showbiz sanctimony. But every second was quintessentially *québécois*: the pro-American but anti-Washington stance, the class consciousness (what other white pop star would not only excuse but *advocate* poor blacks ransacking retail stores?) and the intense identification with New Orleans, which Quebec sees as both a cautionary tale of language loss and a distant-cousin outpost of *joie de vivre* in stiff-necked North America. She shrugged off the million bucks as the least a happy entrepreneur could do, and sang when called upon like the dutiful national daughter ever ready to put her gifts into service.

Because most viewers couldn't see the link between the *nègres blancs* of Quebec and the creole blacks of New

Orleans, Céline's state seemed out of all proportion. But in that light it was as culturally sound as rapper Kanye West's televised outburst the next week that "George Bush doesn't care about black people."

4.
Let's Talk About World Conquest

Céline's passage through the stations of Quebec's *fleur-de-lys*-shaped cross, from shameful hick to emblem of national self-realization, tells one story about what Line Grenier calls the "usefulness of global pop." But it explains less about the *globalness* of global pop; you could argue her rehabilitation at home reflects Quebec's contentment to ride along with the steamroller of Anglo-American monoculture as it flattens the world, mowing down regional cultures like so many hectares of rainforest, clearing ground for a Starbucks at every river mouth and a McDonald's at each desertified crossroads. Indeed, being a stealth operative of globalization is the most substantial charge Quebec intellectuals still lay against her.

If protesters are more likely to cite Arnold Schwarzenegger or Britney Spears in complaints about "Coca-Colonization," they may be too fixated on visuals, because Céline Dion has pierced the global eardrum just as deeply. The process was already well underway by the mid-1990s but the infection went viral when she stowed away on the ultimate planetary love boat, *Titanic*. Upon *Let's Talk About Love*'s international launch, Sony Music Europe's senior vice-president of marketing Richard Ogden told *Music & Media* magazine: "We believe this is the biggest ship-out in the history of Sony Music, bigger even than for Michael Jackson's *HIStory Part 1*." Its $845,000 "kickoff" included a transatlantic video hookup from Céline in Montreal to fans and media in London, Paris and Cologne.

More striking are the anecdotal accounts you'll get from any returning traveler from the developing world, or in a search linking her name with the country of your choice. A sampling:

- Becca Costello, *Sacramento News & Review,* June 30, 2005:

  A few days after my return from a two-week trip to Northern China, a friend asked me, "What's the biggest misconception the Chinese had about the West?" . . . As I struggled to answer my friend's question, I suddenly remembered one misconception I'd encountered often enough to suspect a sort of mass hysteria had settled over the whole country. I lowered my voice and confessed China's shameful secret: "The Chinese believe Céline Dion makes good music." . . . Out of the whole catalog of American, Canadian and British music, the Chinese seem to enjoy primarily four artists: Dion, Mariah Carey, Elton John and Kenny G. Don't mention Madonna. As one university English major told me, 'She's far too scandalous."

- Blogger Michael Dumlao, traveling in Ghana (date unclear):

A la Jesus, Celine is everywhere in Ghana. . . . What is most remarkable about Céline's arachnid reach is that she has managed to appeal to everyone (from stoic chiefs to trend-bucking artisans, pop teens and every single taxi driver in Ghana).

- A February 2007 *USA Today* article credits Céline, Bryan Adams and Lionel Richie with helping popularize Valentine's Day in Ghana, where public displays of affection among unmarried couples are traditionally taboo.

- *Observer Music Magazine*, December 14, 2003, quotes Iraqi twenty-one-year-old Roa'a al Gharab: "There is a lot of pain and separation in Iraqi songs. Generally the Western music we like is slow: Michael Bolton, Celine Dion."

- Richard Lim, entertainment editor of the *Straits Times* in Singapore, May 31, 1998:

  There is no escaping ["My Heart Will Go On"] in Singapore and elsewhere. You hear it in every karaoke lounge, on the radio and in the malls. At her sellout concert at the Indoor Stadium on Wednesday, Taiwanese diva Zhang Huimei included it in her repertoire, and many in the audience sang lustily along with her.

- An NPR piece on the "Changing state of music in Iran" in March 2000, reports on a former opera singer in Tehran, Alahai Hamedi, who at personal risk gives voice lessons to girls, teaching not Iranian or western classical repertoire but songs by Whitney Houston,

Barbra Streisand and Céline.

- In 2000, the *Ottawa Citizen* uncovers documents that reveal that on a 1998 official visit to China, Canadian culture minister Sheila Copps was met with a formal request that Céline tour China. "We followed up," a Canadian press secretary commented, but Céline's staff said it wasn't possible at the time. Copps was there mainly to convince Chinese counterpart Sun Jiazheng to "join the battle" to "ensure cultural diversification in an increasingly globalized world."

- April 21, 2003: The *Chicago Tribune* reports that the most visible cultural influence in Afghanistan was *Titanic*, with Céline in tow. Most residents had seen the movie on illegal video when the Taliban regime was still in place, but now: "In [Kabul's] central market, vendors now sell Titanic Mosquito Killer, Havoc on Titanic Perfume Body Spray, Titanic Making Love Ecstasy Perfume Body Spray. . . . Whatever is big is Titanic. Large cucumbers and potatoes are sold as Titanic vegetables. Popular thick-soled sandals are called Titanic shoes." And Céline tapes played from boomboxes in many stalls.

And that leaves aside all the friends and acquaintances who've told me that in Kazakhstan, Japan, Argentina, wherever, when locals found out they were Canadian, they'd be met with "Ah! Céline Dion!" Is any territory immune to Céline's supposed charms? Well, *Billboard* has reported Sony's frustration at being unable to break her bigger in Germany.

* * *

Unlike most musicians, who establish themselves on a local scene and then aim for wider renown, Céline took the planet for her stage from the beginning. Her 1982 win at the now-defunct Tokyo song contest was succeeded by her bigger victory in 1988 representing Switzerland at the Eurovision Song Contest, the five-decade-old Cheeseball Olympics of pop music, the most-watched ongoing musical event on Earth, with an annual audience estimated at 300 million. Eurovision traffics almost exclusively in major-key, upbeat tunes, limited to three minutes and burdened with somehow simultaneously representing the competing nations' souls and eschewing any hint of chauvinism. Though it began with performers wearing local costume and singing in their native tongues, an "international language" requirement was added in later years by the TV networks that administer it, to make it more commercially viable, so English and French songs predominate. If you've ever seen Italian variety TV, with its blowsy hostesses and pompadoured hosts, you have the general aesthetic. As British Eurovision fan Mike Atkinson wrote in 1996 for Slate.com, "[There] is nothing remotely hip about Eurovision, which generally runs at least 10 years behind developments in youth-based genres, if not 20." Costumes are "florid" and dance routines "frantic," and the prevailing genres are power ballads, bubblegum pop, anthems of international tolerance and what Atkinson calls "'ethereal folksy-ethnic,' which makes much use of Riverdance-style choreography, gypsy fiddles, panpipes and the like." However, as he notes, "this stylistic conservatism does ensure a continuing appeal to the sort of traditional, multigenerational, family-based demographic that is rapidly disappearing in our tightly segmented, multichannel age." Eurovision was made for Céline and she for it. She was the bookies' favorite from the start.

But her world-beating doesn't stop at her status as arguably the world's most-successful talent-show act. She emulated the likes of Whitney Houston by making sure that she had a Hollywood tie-in with each of her 90s English albums: in 1992 it was the title song, with Peabo Bryson, on *Beauty and the Beast*; to boost 1993's *The Color of My Love* she sang "When I Fall in Love" on the soundtrack of *Sleepless in Seattle*; for *Falling into You*, it was *Up Close and Personal*; and of course *Titanic* for *Let's Talk About Love* (though only by a whisker: James Cameron had to be talked into having a theme song, and Céline initially hated "My Heart Will Go On"). Such projects not only enable her to piggyback on the movie-distribution system, they can get her a global audience at the Oscars. Singing at the 1996 Atlanta Olympics had a similar effect.

However, as the University of Leicester's Mashahiro Yasuda points out in his 1999 paper "Localising Dion," Team Céline has gone far beyond those standard means of overseas seduction: they have coordinated with Sony A&R people around the world to tailor singles, bonus tracks and collaborations to each major market. According to a Japanese Sony rep Yasuda interviewed, A. Miyai, early in Céline's career the company decided "no Hollywoodish artist would be possible anymore, apart from the existing ones, such as Michael Jackson"; global markets now demanded another approach. Sony put out a call for ideas to all its offices. In France, it led to Céline's work with Jean-Jacques Goldman. In Japan, where domestic music dominated seventy percent of the market, "The almost unprecedented promotion strategy . . . was to promote Céline

Dion through a network of the Japanese mainstream genre *kayo-kyoku*, which generally relies on an 'image-song' strategy of tie-ins with TV ads and soap operas." A *kayo-kyoku* song is also rushed to karaoke, "which almost systematically excludes international catalogues whose peripheral rights are more complicated to exploit." In 1995 Céline and producer David Foster met the producers of a romantic soap on Fuji TV to create a theme song and "To Love You More," backed by local Sony act Kryzler and Kompany, became the first No. 1 single by a foreigner in Japan in twelve years.

Many other artists would mimic the strategy, but it is only the most dramatic example of Céline being customized to local audiences. When Latin America was a weak point, she began recording songs in Spanish, including *"Amar haciendo el amor,"* included on some editions of *Let's Talk About Love*. Ad campaigns, tours, TV specials and singles are carefully matched with cultural demands. In 1999, when a Céline greatest-hits album was in the works, Sony realized it would have to release several versions to reflect the various Célines belonging to audiences around the world.

She didn't originate this Esperanto-pop capitalism. For that, look to someone like Greece's Nana Mouskouri, whose 60s-to-80s albums were mini-Berlitz courses. But Céline is its modern model citizen, in part because she's not American. Other Canadian songbirds have been particularly keen students, with Shania Twain adding a Bollywoodish "worldbeat" bonus disc to 2002's *Up!* for international markets or Avril Lavigne releasing 2007 hit single *Girlfriend* in eight languages, including Mandarin, and starring in a Japanese *manga* comic. Note that Avril is also on Sony, which is, after all, an Asian concern. The assumption that multinational corporations propagate a western point of view overlooks that increasingly they are not western-based. The Japanese Sony A&R rep told Yasuda that his job was to be "right in front of overseas artists in recording studios, so as to inform them about their Japanese fans and what is expected of them."

Céline has chafed now and then—in 1996, she told *Time*, "I didn't want to do the Spanish song. What do they want me to do next? Learn Japanese?" But two years later, she did sing in Japanese, for another Fuji-TV soap opera. In 1999, after performing on the runway of Hong Kong's decommissioned Kai Tak airport, she was asked at a press conference if she'd be interested in learning Chinese, and answered, "That'd be great! I'd love to learn every language in the world. When you're an artist, a musician, you have a musical ear. It's easier for you to learn languages."

This is becoming the norm, and as Yasuda argues, it's not like the Coca-Colonization stereotype. Now a successful artist has to figuratively *become* local by fulfilling entertainment conventions in other parts of the world. It is less homogenization than hybridization of cultures. As Jan Nedeerveen Pieterse of the Institute of Social Studies in the Hague writes, "How do we come to terms with phenomena such as Thai boxing by Moroccan girls in Amsterdam, Asian rap in London, Irish bagels, Chinese tacos and Mardi Gras Indians in the United States . . . ? Cultural experiences, past or present, have not been simply moving in the direction of cultural uniformity and standardisation." He suggests what we're witnessing is a "creolisation of global culture." It does not follow that creolization will take a standard form. Localism is ignored, as Céline's marketers know, at peril. Likewise the global-hegemony model presumes there won't be reciprocal cultural influence on the west, but the counterevidence is all around us: Asian video-game music, for example, is arguably among the most pervasive influences on young pop musicians now. And as Pieterse points out, with the exception of isolated indigenous groups, civilization and hybridization have been synonymous for centuries.

This is not an answer to exploitation and inequality. But the presumption that the world will automatically become *more like us* is itself chauvinism. Contrary to globalization cheerleader Thomas Friedman's bestselling sloganeering, the world is not going "flat," never has and never will, unless you look through a two-dimensional screen. Yet some western critics of hegemony present merely a negative image of American triumphalism. In George W. Bush's case, it is wishful thinking; in theirs, apocalyptic thinking; but both operate as if the totalization of their own culture were an inevitability, despite all signals of how improbable that is.

* * *

Some of that self-absorption can be heard in the wide-eyed horror with which western witnesses relate Céline's popularity abroad. Local accounts are subtler, indicating how commercial music is redeployed in everyday life for people's own purposes. One of the most astounding tales of Céline's global flexibility comes to me from Jamaican-American music critic Garnette Codogan, who says she may be Jamaica's most popular non-native musical figure. And not just for grandmas.

"I wish I could give you an explanation beyond Jamaicans' love for saccharine tunes, but that may be satisfactory enough," Codogan wrote me.

And the places she turns up in Jamaica are all the more curious. I remember being at sound-system dances and hearing everyone from Bob Marley to Kenny Rogers (yes, Kenny Rogers) to Sade to Yellowman to Beenie Man being blasted at top volume while the crowd danced and drank up a storm. But once the selector (DJ in American parlance) began to play a Céline Dion song, the crowd went buck wild and some people started firing shots in the air. . . . I also remember always hearing Céline Dion blasting at high volume whenever I passed through volatile and dangerous neighborhoods, so much that it became a cue to me to walk, run or drive faster if I was ever in a neighborhood I didn't know and heard Céline Dion mawking over the airwaves.

I sometimes shared this little anecdote with other Jamaican friends, only for them to laughingly comment that they had a similar practice. The unofficial rule seemed to be, "If you hear Céline Dion then you're in the wrong place." That's not to say that roughnecks (as gangsters are also called in Jamaica) are the only ones who appreciate and publicly show their love for Saccharine Céline. It's just that, for some reason, they show her more love than just about any other group.

Codogan asked around, including a few roughnecks, and the reason given was, "to quote one fellow, 'Bad man have fi play love tune fi show 'dat them a lova too.'"

The Pentagon apparently has the same idea. In the run-up to the Iraq war, the US was reported to be wooing Iraqis with a radio station broadcasting Céline to show the west's softer side, alongside Arabic-singing stars, all programmed by Iraqi-American staff in Washington. (Propagandists apparently listen to local informants in a way the occupation forces haven't mastered.) Indeed, comparisons between Céline and Middle Eastern divas surfaced over and over in my research. She may even recognize them herself: An article on the comeback of Iranian superstar Googoosh mentioned Céline attended Googoosh's concert in Toronto.

Yet when reports came out that part of US military intelligence's "no-touch torture" techniques, used to circumvent the Geneva Conventions, include blasting loops of loud music at prisoners night and day—a practice that should sicken any music lover—I came across scads of sniggering downpage editorials and blog posts quipping that "they ought to use Céline Dion": surely *that* would break any recalcitrant P.O.W. In reality, it would be turning some of their favorite music against them. After artist Paul Chan went to Baghdad in 2003 with American activist group Iraqi Peace Team, he told the *Omaha World-Herald* that there, "Everyone loves Celine Dion. For some reason they see her as the pinnacle of sadness. Her songs speak to the plight of the Iraqi people." He added, "It makes me giggle to think that. It makes them more human. And the more human they seem, the harder it is to kill them." It's a patronizing remark, but better than the torture jokes' implication that affection for Céline might as well be a *reason* to kill them.

What's remarkable in many of the stories about Céline's international presence is how moving they are. Think of Chinese gymnast Sang Lan, who was paralyzed in a fall at the 1998 Goodwill Games, and had Céline come to her hospital room in New York and give a private, *a capella* performance. *People* magazine reported: "Says the determined 17-year-old through an interpreter, 'When she goes to Hong Kong next year, I'll find a way to walk there, if that's what it takes.'"

Then there was the Iranian-Canadian activist, Neda Hassani, twenty-six, who immolated herself outside the French embassy in London in June 2003, trying to force the release from French prisons of several leaders of the leftist People's Mujahedeen of Iran, which opposes the Iranian clerical regime. (After her death, some were set free.) The *Ottawa Citizen*'s report of her burial at Pinecrest Cemetery in Ottawa ended, "Amid a glorious pile of wilting flowers laid days before at Ms. Hassani's funeral, a child sang Céline Dion's 'My Heart Will Go On' through a makeshift public-address system, and the tears flowed."

Finally, when I think of how Céline's global impact complicates my sense of her and of the world, I think of another twenty-six-year-old, Mohammed Ahmad Younis, a Baghdad barber. In 2005, he appeared on *Iraq Star*, the Iraqi version of *American Idol,* in which the prize was a record deal—and a ticket out of Iraq. The show was seen as sacrilegious by local militants; contestants were beaten and ostracized. Younis's own girlfriend dumped him for going "too far outside the mainstream." But he still competed, under the pseudonym "Saif from Babylon," because, as he told the *Los Angeles Times*, "I'd rather die and be dead than stay alive and be dead." Wearing sunglasses, a "punk" haircut, fake-leather jeans, platform shoes, blue contact lenses and a black *Star Trek* T-shirt, he performed a tune by Lebanese diva Fairuz, and then encored with "My Heart Will Go On." Promoting him to the next round, one of the judges said, "Good job—I felt as if I was on the *Titanic.*"

Younis must have felt that way, too. Sometimes it seems we're all on that damn boat together.

5.
Let's Talk About Schmaltz

Seattle's Experience Music Project, a hall of pop memora-bilia and interactive music installations, is a metallic blob built by a Microsoft billionaire and a superstar architect to suggest Jimi Hendrix's guitar when seen from the air. It also bleeds money like a Rockefeller on an autopsy table, a flow it's tried to staunch by patching on a sci-fi-movie museum. Perhaps only this space oddity could house the annual EMP Pop Conference, which unites music critics, musicians, professors, industry types and bloggers for three days of warp-factor nerd talk. The 2006 theme was music and shame; it was where I first presented the theme of this book, but it also launched one of the decade's strangest taste controversies, the great "Is Stephin Merritt a racist?" debate. Dozens of warring blog and press commentaries stemmed from the scurrilous claim that the diminutive, gay New York singer from indie-pop project the Magnetic Fields was a sort of crypto-klansman because he said in an EMP plenary that he liked "Zip-a-dee-doo-dah" from Disney's 1946 animated minstrel show *Song of the South*. The detail overlooked by Merritt's self-appointed (and camp-deaf) prosecutors was that he said the cartoon itself was despicable.

But Merritt committed a more genuine gaffe: talking about the studio methods associated with various genres, he said a white, "indie" singer like himself is expected to record with an "authentic"-sounding voice, while massive studio compression and other mediation is expected in "black music, like Céline Dion." Audience members jumped up to point out Céline was neither black nor "black music"; Merritt got slightly flustered, saying he'd misspoken because Céline is produced similarly to R&B divas such as Whitney Houston and Mariah Carey. It was an ironic slip, because Merritt had meant to criticize the subtext of conventions that present "literate" white singers as consciously communicative individuals and (often non-white) "pop" singers more impersonally, like another instrument. Flubbing the personal identity of his example kind of underlined his point.

Still, I don't think it was sheer accident that it was Céline. One of Merritt's online inquisitors spat back that "Céline Dion is unblack as hell," and the locution is telling—the awkward "unblack," not "white as hell." Céline the *Québécoise* falls off the color-coded map of American music, which is part of why global constituencies embrace her. But what does that say about her sound? Though Céline makes forays into R&B and disco, her biggest hits don't match "black music." Neither do they read as "white-as-hell" music, euphemistically genericized as "vanilla." Céline emotes too damply and aggressively to compare to chirpy Pat Boone, the Carpenters or ABBA. She is not mellow or cutesy. So she is not R&B, not vanilla, not "standards/Broadway," not bubblegum, not country, only dabbles in classical "crossover"—what kind of music *is* it?

The only unhyphenated label I can find is "schmaltz." Yet schmaltz is not firmly a genre—it's a descriptor, or an adjective ("schmaltzy") or a verb ("schmaltz it up"), applied to any musical moment of saturated, demonstrative sentiment. But when you come to Céline's American hits, "Because You Loved Me" or "It's All Coming Back to Me Now" or "My Heart Will Go On," schmaltz seems less a quality exhibited than the essential terrain being worked—it functions as an organizing system, as a genre does. If schmaltz is a genre, where does it come from, what is its history? It might help me to hear her if I can place her within a lineage, the way knowing Sidney Bechet's and Lester Young's solos help you decode John Coltrane. But does schmaltz have roots?

* * *

Linguistically it does: *Schmaltz* derives from the German *schmelzen*, "to melt," but it comes into English via Yiddish, as a term for rendered chicken fat. It acquired its American aesthetic meaning thanks to Yiddish-speaking Central European immigrants in the early twentieth century, who brought Yiddish theater to the American stage and then stepped into key roles in vaudeville, Broadway and the rest of New York pop culture. No doubt they would remark to each other that a sentiment-dripping scene or song was too schmaltzy or that an overly dry performance needed more schmaltz, and their non-Jewish collaborators picked it up. There was American popular schmaltz long before the term, but the fact that a non-English word came to name it is consistent with schmaltz's continual coupling with immigration, on the

CARL WILSON

periphery of the central black/white schism of American life. Remember that "white" is a moving target: ethnic groups such as the Irish, Italians, Jews, Poles, Portuguese, francophones, etcetera, eventually became "white," but initially, to their British-descended neighbors, they were not. A genealogy of American schmaltz would probably track neither-black-nor-white cultures through decades of semi-assimilation.

Such a history is beyond me here: it's a field awaiting its scholar. But he or she might begin with nineteenth-century parlor music, which to 2007 ears seems soaked in schmaltz. As detailed in Charles Hamm's invaluable 1979 study *Yesterdays*, popular song in America was first dominated by the songs sung in English pleasure gardens: airs from operettas, comic songs, sunny courtship tunes. (I'm distinguishing "popular" from "folk," which could be more rough-and-tumble and so didn't get the same public berth. Nicholas Tawa makes the case in his 1980 book, *Sweet Songs for Gentle Americans: The Parlor Song in America, 1790–1860,* with the best quick definition of pop music ever: "[Parlor song's] creation and its performances were intended for no one particular. Its introduction to the public was a speculation on the part of all those involved that large numbers of people would sponsor it.") Along with piano arrangements of classical music, parlor songs were the main occupation of the early sheet-music business, which evolved into the music publishing and eventually recording industries. They were sung not only at home but in professional concerts, variety shows and theatricals.

But then parlor song was changed by Thomas Moore's eight-volume *Irish Melodies*, published between 1808 and 1834, which brought less genteel, even lachrymose sounds and subjects to American music. Hamm suggests the *Irish*

Melodies introduced *nostalgia* as a central nineteenth-century musical and literary theme: amid America's piety and mercantile go-getterism, it unearthed the kernel of uneasy rootlessness shared by a nation of immigrants, using an immigrant musical strain.

The other major rival to British music in nineteenth-century America matters a lot in finding Céline Dion's musical roots: Italian opera. Through most of that century, opera was popular music, too, sung on the same programs as parlor songs and beloved among both high and low economic classes in English translation. Rossini, Bellini and Donizetti (and the occasional Viennese, such as Mozart) were sensations when fitted to English lyrics, and arias were huge sheet-music hits, sung domestically with all the Italian vocal flourishes (*portamento, fioritura, melisma*) that would later be the stuff of uncool "oversinging" in American pop. Operatic songs, full of melodrama and romance, were sung alongside parlor songs at home and parlor songs would be dropped into productions of operas (often when rowdily participatory nineteenth-century audiences yelled out for them). Swedish soprano Jenny Lind's mid-century American tour, sponsored by P. T. Barnum, was perhaps the first "blockbuster" event in American pop culture, and Lind would sing "Yankee Doodle Dandy" between Mozart and hymns. Parodies of opera arias were standard fare even in nineteenth-century minstrel shows, the words twisted into the pidgin "negro" speech invented by blackface comedians, as Lawrence Levine chronicles in his crucial study *Highbrow/Lowbrow: The Emergence of Cultural Hierarchy in America* (1988). The same held true for passages of Shakespeare, another popular nineteenth-century commodity. It was only in the later 1800s that a consolidating upper class became wealthy and populous enough to shut out populist treatments of classics in the name of "culture" and "standards," by building ritzy exclusive opera houses, condemning English translations and turning against "light" Italian opera in favor of "high" German opera. This brought to an end the mixed programs of Shakespeare, opera, melodrama, parlor song, comedy, freak shows and acrobats typical of the earlier ninteenth-century stage. As Walt Whitman, an enormous Italian-opera fan, put it in 1871's *Democratic Vistas*, with "this word Culture, or what it has come to represent, we find ourselves abruptly in close quarters with the enemy," meaning the snobs and aristocrats of old Europe.

But these "foreign" influences left indelible marks on American pop music. Hamm writes: "In a very real sense, the concept of popular song may be said to have begun with Henry Russell [1812–1901, "Woodman Spare That Tree," "The Old Armchair"]—an English-born Jew who studied in Italy, first came to Canada and then furnished Americans with songs in an Italian musical style, mostly to texts reflecting an Irish type of nostalgia. Of such ethnic mixtures was popular song in America born." The same could be said of the greatest American songwriter of that century, Stephen Foster, who added to English, Irish and Italian stylings his own Scottish background and the purportedly African-American rhythms and harmonies of the minstrel stage.

Lyrically, aside from the novelty/comic numbers, later parlor music was a torrent of schmaltz. "American singers valued most those compositions that stressed 'the sentiments of the heart'," writes Tawa. "An indispensable function of parlor song was the reflection and reinforcement of values shared by most Americans." They were full of scorned maidens, sainted mothers, heroic soldiers and dead wives and babies. To a modern audience "less disposed to expose their emotions to public scrutiny," nearly all of them "verge on mawkishness."

And that is the way American popular music remained into the twentieth century, when Tin Pan Alley, dominated by more assimilated Jews, changed the tone: Suddenly popular song aimed at an up-and-coming urban-industrial listenership, most of all in New York, on Broadway. It took on a brash sophistication that eschewed the schmaltzy excesses of the past century and most of the Italianate ornamentation, relying for spice instead on borrowings from brass bands, South American dances, the emerging jazz and European modernism. Even sentimental Tin Pan Alley standards were likely to express feeling in subtler harmonic progressions, not weepy crescendos and plaints, and to use plays on words and up-to-date slang, reflecting keen competition among the closely quartered Manhattan songwriting clique. It went over thanks to the new audience of city slickers, but also because radio and recording made more fragmented marketing possible—rural and southern people availed themselves of the new "hillbilly" (folk and country) and "race" (blues and later R&B) recordings, and Hamm argues that Tin Pan Alley's half-century of pop dominance was never wholly embraced by those listeners (though they took it in at the movies and in country or R&B versions of the songs). Country and blues were more heart-on-sleeve musics that never fully adapted the archness and on-the-make spirit of the citified mainstream.

* * *

Even in cities, though, there were exceptions. Al Jolson was a schmaltz merchant and so was his fellow Yiddish-stage vet Sophie Tucker, though they both balanced the menu with a heavy helping of comedy. Tenor Enrico Caruso was the first smash vocal-recording artist, showing Italian opera could still capture twentieth-century audiences (though less and less frequently). Irish tenor John McCormack made a Jenny Lind-sized impression as a visiting ballad singer. And throughout the Tin Pan Alley era there would be occasional soppier hits (Erno Rapee's 1933 "Charmaine," Harry Warren's 1934 "I Only Have Eyes For You," Danny DiMinno and Carmen Lombardo's 1937 "Return to Me"), again from the pens of immigrant songwriters (Warren was Italian). As Tawa notes in his 1982 book on immigration and American music, *A Sound of Strangers*: "The ethnic American singers who popularized songs like the ones cited—such vocalists as Tony Bennett, Dean Martin, Tony Martin, Perry Como, Vic Damone, Al Jolson, Julius La Rosa, Al Martino and Frank Sinatra—were specialists at manipulating all the emotional stops for putting over a song." Many of them were versatile enough to put over cool jazz standards too, but unlike most of their white singing-star counterparts, they had no compunction about slipping into an oozing bath of schmaltz.

Céline Dion's music and career are more understandable if she is added to the long line of ethnic "outsiders" who expressed emotions too outsized for most white American performers but in non-African-American codes, letting white audiences loosen up without crossing the "color line." It's easy to overlook the likes of 1950s tenor superstar Mario Lanza, the self-styled Caruso heir who fell out with the elite opera due to his career in Hollywood melodramas but sold millions upon millions of pop-opera records in the 1950s. Or

Jerry Vale (born Genaro Louis Vitaliano), who had hits with Italian-language pop gushers around the same time. Even in instrumental music, the syrupy sounds of string sections, piano kitsch and "sweet jazz" were for many years dominated by people with names like Annunzio Mantovani, Liberace and Guy Lombardo (scorned by collectors of "hot jazz" like Louis Armstrong's, though Satchmo himself thought Lombardo had the best band in America).

But schmaltz also took some unexpected postwar turns: Country broke out of the hillbilly ghetto and, though it included the rawer tones of Hank Williams or Johnny Cash (no strangers to schmaltz), it exposed a surviving Southern strain of nineteenth-century parlor song, in ballads by the likes of Jim Reeves and Marty Robbins, a connection going back to the Carter Family and opera-trained 1920s cowboy singer Vernon Dalhart. Elvis Presley, often namechecked by Céline (many *Québécois* make fervent pilgrimages to Graceland), united country-schmaltz with his idolization of Italian crooners when he sang the ballads that broadened his popularity beyond the bobbysoxers, such as "Are You Lonesome Tonight?," "Love Me Tender" (to the tune of Civil War song "Aura Lee") and later "It's Now or Never" (adapted from 1898 Neapolitan song "O Sole Mio"). The Vegas Elvis foretold the coming of Vegas Céline; the King of Rock'n'Roll was also Prince of Schmaltz. Outside the United States, European schmaltz specialists also made a global impact in the postwar era, such as Greece's Nana Mouskouri and the French balladeers Maurice Chevalier and Charles Aznavour. The Quebec variety tradition from which Céline hails was heavily influenced by them. But most are a degree more modest and quaint than American schmaltz.

During the 1960s, soul and folk balladry pushed schmaltz to the back burner. Much is made of Céline's hero-worship of Barbra Streisand, but often I don't hear the resemblance in classic Barbra: A Broadway-bred baby, her self-conscious comic timing allowed her to dance on the edge of the grease pan without sliding in. She began to get schmaltzier only as the style returned from the repressed in the 1970s and 1980s, by which I mean not the vanilla ultrasensitivity of Bread, but the nostalgic showmanship of Barry Manilow or Neil Diamond, who repeated Tin Pan Alley and its prehistory in a mode of over-the-top farce. There also arose the special flavors of rock-meeting-schmaltz known as the power ballad (to which we'll return in the next chapter), as well as the Eurotrash hash of schmaltz and rock in Andrew Lloyd Webber (think of "Memory" from *Cats*). And "Latin" balladeers made a come-back with melted-cheese idols such as Julio Iglesias. Céline and her producers have extracted all the most concentrated emotional elixirs, from opera to parlor song to arena rock, and blended them into a recipe for hyperschmaltz, a Frankengenre of sentimental intensity.

In a conversation about Céline's precedents with other music critics and big-eared fans on an email list, someone remarked, "I don't think this particular Cinderella wears American sizes." If you look only to gowns cut and fashioned in the Anglo- and African-American mainstreams, she has a point; but the kind of schmaltz-Americana in which Céline partakes has been a continuing strain in US popular music for two centuries, whether or not the people performing it were fully counted as American. Schmaltz circles the rim but seemingly never wholly dissolves in the melting pot, bubbling up again decade after decade.

I think this is because schmaltz, as Hamm insinuates in his discussion of parlor song, is never purely escapist: it is not just cathartic but socially reinforcing, a vicarious exposure to both the grandest rewards of adhering to norms and their necessary price. This makes it especially vulnerable to becoming dated: the outer boundaries of extreme conformity, of uncontroversial public ecstasy and despair, are ever-mobile. Schmaltz is an unprivate portrait of how private feeling is currently conceived, which social change can pitilessly revise. And then it becomes shameful, the way elites of the late nineteenth century felt when they wondered what their poor ignorant forbears ever heard in light Italian opera. Likewise, as a specialization of liminal immigrants in America, it can become a holdover from a time "before we were white," perhaps dotingly memorialized, but embarrassing head-on. Schmaltz rots faster than other ingredients in the musical pantry, which may be why we doubt the possibility of a Céline Dion revival in 2027, just as a craze for Jerry Vale's 1956 "Innamorata" seems unlikely now. Is a genre automatically lesser, artistically and in social function, for being more perishable? Is it best to keep the schmaltz drained off of art (unlike the freaks-to-ballads-to-Shakespeare plurality of the nineteenth-century stage) or is a cooler, drier musical place one where some fundamental human need has been left to shrivel? Under the surface of popular music, greasing its rails, the secret history of schmaltz runs on in oleaginous currents, awaiting deeper exploration.

6.
Let's Sing Really Loud

Few items in pop-music history are as fetishized as the "lost album," recordings that go unreleased because the label (or the artist) lost faith, the artist had a breakdown, the band broke up. . . . The Beach Boys' *Smile* is the most storied, but there's also the Who's *Lifehouse*, Neil Young's *Homegrown*, two or three Prince albums and many more (even by more obscure bands, like the Mountain Goats with *Hail and Farewell Gothenberg*), each one much speculated on, bootlegged where possible, and in *Smile*'s case remade in facsimile decades later. It's hard to separate this from a romanticism that regards albums as an auteur medium, like an Old Masters painting in which every song is another brushstroke. So I was caught off guard to learn there is in fact a "lost" Céline Dion album, or at least partial album—her 1995 sessions with producer Phil Spector, the architect of the early-1960s Wall of Sound who turned girl-group hits into "teenage symphonies to God"; controversial collaborator with the Beatles, Leonard Cohen and the Ramones; and, at the moment, murder suspect.

Spector was fired as one of the producers of *Falling into You*, which would have been his first record in fifteen years. Questioned by *Entertainment Weekly* in 2003, Spector responded with an eight-hundred-word letter condemning the "contrived and repugnant" material imposed on Céline by other producers, "Whitney Houston- and Mariah Carey-rejected, soundalike songs . . . 'produced' by amateurs, students and bad clones of yours truly." (Céline's camp said Spector just took too much time; behind the scenes, self-professed "bad clone" Jim Steinman said the sessions had been "a pretty hilarious nightmarish experience.") Spector told *EW* that "should you wish to hear the amazing and historic recordings I have made with Ms. Dion, have no fear. . . . Since I paid for them and own them, I am planning to release them on my label, for the entire world to hear and compare." No one familiar with René Angelil's lawyers' grip on all things Céline will be surprised that four years later not a note has come to light. But it could be revelatory: as her French work with Jean-Jacques Goldman has shown, astute production and repertoire advice can have a dramatic effect. Céline herself has said, "I couldn't give [Spector] the time he wanted, and it's too bad because, believe me, the songs were just unbelievable."

I was just struck that Spector had worked with her in the first place. For decades he has broken seclusion only for artists he thought worthy, anointed innovators such as Cohen or the Ramones. In his 2003 letter, he had only praise for Céline herself. So Spector regards Céline as every bit the singer, indeed the artist, that she's made out to be. And he's not alone. *Elle* magazine reported in 2007 that Prince had been to her Vegas show at least three times, joining the likes of Rick Rubin (producer of various rap legends along with Johnny Cash),

Ice-T, Justin Timberlake (less of a surprise) and Alice Cooper. Hip-hop and R&B producer Timbaland told *Elle*, "Céline has such a beautiful, mesmerizing voice." R&B singer R. Kelly, who has dueted with Céline, proclaimed himself "an absolute, wouldn't-be-embarrassed, chase-the-bus-down fan. Her voice is, like, *not human* . . . " It's not uncommon for musicians to bypass taste categories when they hear technical achievement, and Céline seems to be such a case.

Of course, her career is dedicated to the proposition that her voice was not created equal. In *Saturday Night Live*'s parody, Ana Gasteyer's Céline greets the audience, "I am French-Canadian, I am really skinny, and guess what, I am the best singer in the world!" She adds: "If I wasn't such a nice person, I'd think I was a showoff." The music writer Barry Mazor, who has a fine palate for classic American schmaltz, once told me he heard Céline as "investing Primary Narcissism with a voice." And that was just it for me: her vocal presentation called to mind a two-year-old the universe must revolve around, importuning "look at me!" in escalating volumes and key changes until its tantrum-like climax. The showboating rendered the voice moot, as half of great singing is in knowing when to hold back.

But as I've investigated, this impression keeps running up against a counternarrative, the one in which Céline's vocal personality is completely rewritten by different producers, in which she seems almost a vocal submissive. Talk to people about Céline Dion and, whether they like her or not, they'll acknowledge her vocal ability, but the word you hear most often is "pipes"—as if she were a conveyance system, a set of tubes to pump music through, more a feat of engineering than a person. Céline speaks of herself much the same way: one of the recurrent themes is the self-discipline required to care for her voice, whether by going for days without speaking and communicating to her husband in hand signals, or spending enormous sums on regulating temperature and humidity in her residences and dressing rooms (especially in the desert of Las Vegas). You could call this narcissism or see it as a very Catholic self-abnegation—the vow of silence, the withdrawals, as if her voice were a higher power for which she's only the host. You know, "the voice of an angel."

* * *

The two most carefully considered critiques I have read about Céline's work, both printed in the *Village Voice*, centered on this opposition between voice and identity. In 2002, in a half-positive review of *A New Day Has Come*, Frank Kogan wrote that while he often enjoyed her music, he had "never heard a distinct musical personality in it. Being a pop star isn't just about hitting the high notes; it's about making people feel they're hearing *you* in those high notes, or so I assumed. . . . There was a primal leviathan of *something*, but it failed to engulf me."

Five years earlier, Simon Frith's review of *Let's Talk About Love* drilled into the gulf between Céline and her duet partner Barbra Streisand, whom he credited with "an intellectual arrogance." Céline, by contrast, despite her "remarkable ability to draw attention to the emotional weight of a single note," lacked "any sense of personality." Frith concluded: "Barbra Streisand found new ways of selling classic songs, making something individual and obdurate out of them; Céline Dion is given songs written to sell her. . . . The result is a strangely passive music: hear Streisand impose herself on a song; hear Dion let the song shape her identity."

I have been trying to imagine why, to some listeners, to Céline herself, this might be a good thing. Why, like a gambler addicted to losing, Céline seems so eerily eager to disperse herself into her music, squandering more than the surplus until nothing remains but special effects: all that is solid melts into schmaltz.

"My work," she once said, "is to enter people's lives with my music. Do you think I want to disturb them when they bake? Do you think I want to disturb them when they make love? I want to be part of it. I don't want to interrupt. One thing that I didn't want to do is to push *me*—I am this, I am that, I'm for this and not for that, listen to this, believe in this. I'm doing my job, my song, and if you want to hear this song and not that song, I have nothing to do with it."

Céline's main form, the power ballad, was the 1970s' arena-rock invention that did most to recover the schmaltz impulse after its 1960s exile from pop's main street. As we're reminded by her covers of such anthems of isolation as Eric Carman's "All By Myself" and Leo Sayer's "When I Need You," the power ballad is the moment when the singer ventures onto the lip of the stage and the band steps back. Seldom has a soloist been so part of a team as Céline Dion, but when she sings a ballad she is alone with the hulking presence of her voice, even as the lyrics refer constantly back to themes of interpersonal connection and love. The dynamic is perfectly tailored for a teen avoiding homework with her face in the pillow, headphones on. Or the widow whose loneliness is the underside of a sense-memory of togetherness. Or the suburban homemaker pausing beside the radio holding a cup of coffee, with everyone else out at school or work. In tending to her voice as if she had nothing to do with it, Céline reproduces the maternal sacrifice of Maman Dion, musically incarnates the woman who takes care of everybody but herself. The masochistic devotion proclaimed in so many of the songs presents a martyr persona, with its paradoxical mix of self-destruction and self-glorification. If she sings without personality it is because it would be selfish of her to come not so much between listener and song but between the listener and her own voice.

Psychology and philosophy today often question whether there is such a thing as the core self, or only a shifting social self-reassemblage, "bricolage with no bricoleur." Céline's blankness simulates that model musically: her songs disclose little personality because she is just the voice's vessel, all medium and no message, channeling feeling impeded by as few contours as possible, streaming light into her fans' lives. No wonder they often speak of her in terms of saintliness and maternal care. This ego vacuum makes her seem phony to her detractors—lacking the expressive individuality Stephin Merritt said his fans expected—but perhaps it seems more *honest* to her devotees that she presents a subjectivity so flimsy and precarious, as all subjectivity can be. The authenticity is in the gift, not the giver. Perhaps the receiver feels honored by this, a bit more solid herself.

Yet this makes for an unusual absence of musical tension. As her songs rocket to their predestined apexes, she does not resist, she goes along for the ride, leaning on the accelerator and seldom the brake, emphasizing intensity not difference. It reminds me of nothing so much as current "underground" metal, which has thrown out the spare musical parts of past

CARL WILSON

hard rock and pared down to loud guitars, drums and screaming. Today's metal has no power ballads, no more Nazareth
doing 'Love Hurts,' no more Kiss doing 'Beth,' no more
Guns N' Roses' 'Sweet Child o' Mine.' So Céline is singing
them instead. It's been said that "pro wrestling is soap opera
on steroids," so maybe Céline Dion is metal on estrogen.
And metal, remember, has now been admitted to the critical
sanctum. Metal is all darkness and rebellion and Céline all
candlelight and communion, but note how hypermasculinity
and hyperfeminity in this way can meet, like plutocratic capitalism and command-economy communism. When people
joke that Céline is like a drag queen, perhaps it's this aspect of
her music, not just her pointed features, that prompts it.

For listeners attuned to the history of popular music,
Céline's let-me-take-you-higher (and louder) drive is puzzling
because it reverses how vocal technique has followed recording technology. The earliest singers on cylinder recordings,
from the parlor tradition or the vaudeville stage, had an operatic, belting quality. But as microphone science was refined,
this gave way to the gentler "croon" associated with singers
such as Bing Crosby; in contemporary R&B you hear the cul-
mination of that process with singers who flutter in and out
of the frame in *oohs, aahs* and whispers while beats and loops
fill the space. This trend has never been unidirectional, with
singers coming out of high-volume live contexts like electric
blues and rock, the Broadway stage and the gospel church (the
background of most African-American pop divas) regularly
reviving top-of-the-lungs options. But even those performers
tend gradually to tone down to fewer theatrics, closer to the
level of speech. Céline seems to go big for fewer apparent
reasons. Maybe she's just a creature of the era of studio com-

pression, in which records clamoring to be heard have been mastered at higher decibel levels year by year. But there may be a less technical explanation.

I think back to her outburst on the New Orleans looters, "*Let them touch those things!*" I've come to hear it as Céline's one-line manifesto. The overgrown sonics of her music, what you might call *conspicuous production*, are there so that she, the poor girl from Charlemagne, can touch them. Like hip-hop, it's aspirational music, about getting paid, though Céline, as culture and gender dictate, is more demure about it. Her voice is a luxury item, and Céline wants to share its abundance with her audience, wants them to be able to touch and be touched by it, by its ornamental melisma and plush velvet AutoTuning and its many octaves like the wings of a mansion. Her singing itself is aspirational, reaching out palpably in vocal curlicues and unfurling bolts, like overstuffed furniture festooned with a fat flower pattern. Her voice itself is *nouveau riche*. It's a volume business. No wonder middle-class critics find it gauche.

To supposedly more refined, educated ears, being a "showoff" is the height of tackiness. But for anyone with normal aspirations to get ahead, even modestly, the choice in the "artier" side of popular music not to play or sing obviously well can be just as unfathomable: most performers can't "afford" to make that decision, figuratively or literally. It's certainly uncommon in black American music (even hip-hop, for all its subcultural semi-refusals, still puts a premium on signs of mastery, from flow to ho's). And contrary to urban outsiders' frequent misconceptions, singing out of tune or playing ineptly has always been taboo in country music. (As John Sebastian sang, "Nashville cats get work before they're two.") All the heirs of Bob Dylan who downplay conventional

CARL WILSON

musicality in order to isolate what Roland Barthes called "the grain of the voice," another order of meaning and materiality, are explicitly disdaining standard measures of entertainment value and the ambitions they represent. Céline pays such aspirations tribute in every note.

The word "virtuosity" is rooted, after all, in *virtue*. There is the classical model in which virtuosity is taken almost as given, by "virtue" of proper upbringing and training. But in pop it bespeaks a work ethic, which serves to rationalize the indulgence of musical pleasure. A display of skill in a guitar or drum solo is the confirming ritual of blue-collar rock (which made it the *bête noir* of punk). The disciplinary regimes surrounding Céline's voice fascinate her fans, and while for Céline they may have a Catholic overtone, they also fit the American Gnostic Christian notion that devoting yourself to work (to a degree that would be greedily unseemly in many cultures) can be part of your personal relationship to God, investing your "talents," your store of divinely appointed currency.

* * *

Her virtue gives Céline a special place as a role model for aspiring singers. Given her Eurovision and Tokyo victories, you could almost say the talent show, more than any other genre, constitutes her roots. Her name is invoked wherever *American Idol*–style singing contests take place, especially by the white female singers on the TV show, but equally by contestants in Chicago's expatriate vocal competition *Abyssinian Star* and similar events around the world. Katherine Meizels, a conservatory-trained singer and California-based scholar studying *American Idol*, told me that among *Idol* judges, "A comparison to Céline is sometimes made when judges approve of a contestant's performance. [But] when contestants sing Céline's songs, much of the time they are chastised for being overambitious." When contestant Antonella Barba (who eventually dropped out because dirty pictures of her hit the Internet) sang "Because You Loved Me" in the semifinals of Season 6, judge Paula Abdul warned, "Less than one per cent of the population can sing like Céline." (Meizels wondered, "Did she do a scientific study?")

American Idol attracts critical venom almost as much as Céline herself, and for many of the same reasons: For all the show's concentration on character and achievement, it is not about the kind of self-expression critics tend to praise as real. It celebrates, as Meizels pointed out, what cultural-studies writer Lawrence Grossberg has called "authentic inauthenticity," the sense of showbiz known and enjoyed as a *genuine fake*, in a time when audiences are savvy enough to realize image-construction is an inevitability and just want it to be fun. "Authentic inauthenticity" is really just another way of saying "art," but people caught up in romantic ideals still bristle to admit how much of creativity is being able to manipulate artifice. Rock musicians often disguise showmanship as spontaneous passion or profound symbolism (Pink Floyd's giant inflatable pig) or a sincere, "fourth-wall-breaking" contact between stage and crowd (a punk singer spits at you; Green Day pulls audience members up and hands them the instruments). But the tricks always aim at magic anyway. And many people are happy to subscribe to the pop singer-as-illusionist. The "big voice" is very showbiz in this sense. In the case of a singer like Céline, some of the intoxication is in the sensation that she is at once doing tricks with her voice and is herself overwhelmed by its natural force: Her virtuosity is simultaneously slight-of-hand and somehow *real* magic, a kind of vocal sublime, a mighty waterfall inspiring fear and awe. With virtuous effort she channels the waterfall through the "pipes," so we get the head rush, but not the threat of inundation.

Luxurious anonymity, virtuous excess, sincere illusion, metal on estrogen, a safeguarded sublime—all these undertones to Céline's voice seem almost tangible to me, and yet in my (backstage) listening so far to *Let's Talk About Love*, I cannot quite touch these things. In Frank Kogan's review he writes, "I felt right to be unengulfable, but not right to be ignorant about the nature of the engulfment. Twenty-eight million people can be wrong, but they're not all likely to allow themselves to be bored." By this halfway mark in my experiment, for all the sense I've been able to make of Céline, why am I still bored? The answers may lie not in our pop star, but in ourselves.

7.
Let's Talk About Taste

So far I've been re-examining global pop, schmaltz, big-voiced singing and other aspects of Céline's career from unaccustomed angles, finding thirteen ways of looking at a songbird, circling to try to find a more objective standpoint. But is there any objectivity to be found in artistic taste? The debate over whether beauty lies solely in the eye of the beholder runs through cultural history. It arises every time a critic makes a top ten list: Am I just naming the movies or books or albums I liked most in the preceding year, or am I asserting these ten works somehow were *in fact* the best or most significant? Do I dare to say the two claims are related?

Less trivially, "objectivity" is in play whenever there is a court case of censorship that results in art experts being summoned to testify to the "merit" of the transgressing work. These opinions are treated as *evidence*, as if they came from a forensic report—except that the prosecutors also bring out their own professors, curators or critics to argue that the accused creation is in fact devoid of redeeming aesthetic or social value. The verdict often turns on which experts have more prestige, making their tastes more *believable*: If one set comes from small Christian schools and the other from Harvard and Oxford, you can guess the outcome. A string of such spectacles took place in the late 80s and early 90s when neoconservatives took aim at record companies for putting out heavy metal and rap albums that offended "family values" and at the National Endowment for the Arts for granting public funding to "obscene" art. These "culture wars" preoccupied arts advocates for nearly a decade. They could as easily have been called taste wars.

One of the most trenchant responses came from a duo of immigrant artists, Russian expatriates Vitaly Komar and Alexandir Melamid: if the problem is what standards of taste ought to prevail in a diverse and democratic society, they asked, why not decide by democracy's best approximation of "objectivity," a popular vote? Since a taste election is difficult to imagine, Komar and Melamid (previously known for their satires on official Soviet socialist-realist art) settled for other thermometers of the public temperature: opinion polls and focus groups. They commissioned an $80,000 "People's Choice" poll asking Americans what they liked and didn't like in art—sizes, styles, subjects, colors—and proceeded to make two paintings: "America's Most Wanted" and "America's Most Unwanted."

The poll spoke loud and clear: America liked the color blue, and images of natural landscapes, historical figures, women and children and/or large mammals on midsized canvases. So Komar and Melamid produced a "dishwasher-sized" picture of rolling hills, blue skies and blue water beside which a family is picnicking while George Washington, a deer and a hippopotamus stand idly by. The "Most Unwanted" painting is a small, sharp-angled geometric abstract in gold and orange. They conducted smaller polls around the world: *every country* wanted a blue landscape.

The laughs here aren't just at the expense of popular taste. As Melamid said in an interview in the book *Painting by Numbers: Komar and Melamid's Scientific Guide to Art* (1997):

> There's a crisis of ideas in art, which is felt by many, many people. . . . Artists now—I cannot speak for all, but I have talked to many artists who feel this way—we have lost even our belief that we are the minority that *knows*. We believed ten years ago, twenty years ago, that we knew the secret. Now we have lost this belief. We are a minority with no power and no belief, no faith. I feel myself, as an artist and as a citizen, just totally obsolete. . . . Okay, it can be done this way or that way or this way, or in splashes or smoothly, but why? What the hell is it about? That's why we wanted to ask people. For us—from our point of view—it's a sincere thing to understand something, to change the course. Because the way we live we cannot live anymore. I have never seen artists so desperate as they are now, in this society.

Added Komar, in his accented English:

> Also, art world is not democratic society, but totalitarian one. It does not have checks and balances. Individuals who create its laws and criteria are also its main decision-makers. This conflation of executive, legislative and judiciary is hallmark of totalitarian society.

In collaboration with New York composer and neuro-scientist Dave Soldier, they also conducted a smaller-scale, Internet survey to produce the People's Choice Music. The uproarious "Most Unwanted Song" turned out to be, as dictated by the poll, more than twenty-five minutes long, included accordions, bagpipes, a children's choir, banjo, flute, tuba and synthesizer (the only instrument in both the most wanted and most unwanted tunes) and mashed up opera, rap, Muzak, atonal music, advertising jingles and holiday songs. The "Most Wanted Song," the song that would be "unavoidably and uncontrollably 'liked' by seventy-two percent, plus or minus twelve percent, of listeners," was a five-minute R&B slow jam, a male-female duet with guitar, sax, drums, synths and strings. Critics often described it as sounding like . . . Céline Dion. And they all claimed to like the "Most Unwanted" much better.

Is Céline Dion's music a dishwasher-sized blue landscape? And if a statistically solid majority of the Earth's people, plus or minus twelve percent, wanted to fill the world with sappy love songs, what would be wrong with that? Who gets to say? Komar and Melamid were addressing a widespread collapse of faith in all regimes of taste that previously guided not only the reception but the making of art. As refugees from a totalitarian state, they were earnest about democracy; as artists, they understood (as their project inevitably demonstrates) that the mechanisms of democracy are hopeless for art. No individual person would actually want the "Most Wanted Painting," a ridiculous jumble of incongruent elements. It was a sincerely painful joke about art and democracy—as is the history of taste, for anyone who takes both democracy and art seriously.

Komar and Melamid's pseudoscientific project is a reminder that science so far has little to say about taste. Evolutionary theorists propose the blue-landscape ideal may derive from an embedded longing for the primeval savannah, and that admiration for musical virtuosity has to do with its function as sexual-status display, like a bird's bright plumage. Anthropology finds social music (for dancing, religious rites, parties, relating stories) in all human cultures; music for "pure" listening is an anomaly. And brain science has shown how musical pleasure is structured by expectation and familiarity, in a particular song (when will the pattern resolve, and how?), between songs (is this music like other music we know and like?) and between genres (do you know the rules of this kind of music?). Balancing repetition and novelty is crucial: some songs feel too complicated to enjoy (like the "Most Unwanted" song) and others too clichéd to hold interest (as critics found the "Most Wanted"). There's little explanation, though, of why people gravitate toward different ratios of surprise to familiarity. Going by the patrons of experimental music concerts, people who like formally unpredictable art are not especially prone to drive fast cars, bungee jump or even talk to strangers. But they do seem more likely also to be reading obscure novels or looking at weird paintings. Is there a "risk gene" for artistic adventurousness?

The new discipline of musical neurobiology, well outlined in Montreal researcher (and ex-record producer) Daniel Levitin's *This Is Your Brain on Music* (2006), hints that the brain might be built to prefer consonance to dissonance, steady rhythms over chaotic ones and so forth. However, these penchants seem to be malleable, as science journalist Jonah Lehrer says in *Proust Was a Neuroscientist*

(2007). There's a network of neurons in the brain stem specifically geared to sort unfamiliar sounds into patterns. When they succeed, the brain releases a dose of pleasure-giving dopamine; when they fail, when a sound is *too* new, excess dopamine squirts out, disorienting and upsetting us. Lehrer suggests this explains events such as the 1913 riots at the Paris premiere of Igor Stravinsky's dissonant *The Rite of Spring*. But these neurons also *learn*. With repeated exposure, they can tame the unknown, turn "noise" back into "music." Thus, a year later, another Parisian audience cheered for *The Rite of Spring* and in 1940, Walt Disney put it in a children's cartoon, *Fantasia* (appropriately enough, the dinosaurs-and-evolution sequence).

The problem with this parable is that it isn't really about repeated exposure. Maybe the brains of children in *Fantasia*'s audience were readied by having heard music influenced by Stravinsky. But what about the 1914 audience? It seems implausible it was mainly the rioters returning to give him a second chance. No, it would have been the hipsters of 1914, lured by the *succès de scandale* and *eager* to be shocked, to take the dopamine overdose. Their neurons were prepared without ever hearing the sounds. The picture is fuzzy unless we can measure the effect of received concepts and social identifications on "private" neuro-auditory processes.

Still, the field is young. I wouldn't be surprised if variances in individual brain chemistry help explain taste predilections: if Céline fans and I disagree on whether her music is fresh, maybe my brain is a bigger dopamine junkie. Likewise, that the ranks of *outré*-music aficionados are so full of the socially awkward suggests their nonconformism may not be entirely by choice. (*Artistic, autistic*—watch your pronunciation.)

But the bias that "conformity" is a pejorative has led, I think, to underestimating the part mimesis—imitation—plays in taste. It's always other people following crowds, whereas my own taste reflects my specialness. A striking demonstration of the mimetic effect comes from a group of Columbia University sociologists, who took advantage of the Internet as a zone in which you can conduct large-scale simulations of mass-culture behavior, isolated from advertising and other distorting factors. They set up a website (as researcher Duncan J. Watts explains in a 2007 *New York Times Magazine* article) called Music Lab, where 14,000 registered participants were asked to "listen to, rate and, if they chose, download songs by bands they had never heard of." One group could see only song titles and band names; the rest were divided into eight "worlds," and could see which songs in their "world" were most downloaded. In these "social-influence worlds," as soon as a song generated a few downloads, more people began downloading it. Higher-rated songs did do somewhat better, but each world had different "hits," depending which songs "caught on" there first. They called the effect "cumulative advantage," a rule that popularity tends to amplify exponentially. (In the control group, quality ratings and popularity usually matched.) Does this mean people are lemmings? No, just that we're social: we are curious what everybody else is hearing, want to belong, want to have things in common to talk about. We are also insecure about our own judgments and want to check them against others. So songs might in part be famous simply for being famous. Intriguingly, as Watts notes, "Introducing social influence into human decision making . . . didn't just make the hits bigger; it also made them more unpredictable."

Perhaps cumulative advantage's semirandomized conformity helps explain why the history of art is not all blue landscapes. When "early adopters" help make a Picasso famous, his reputation becomes self-inflating; the mutation becomes the mainstream, even though few people immediately like his paintings. Taste's insecurity turns out to be the prerequisite for artistic growth.

Aesthetics is the discipline created to contend with this insecurity, but considering that philosophy of art has been underway for at least three centuries (since the Enlightenment, and much longer if you include Aristotle), it comes up quite short on accounting for taste. It has analyzed elegantly the myriad ways the elements of art function, but when it confronts conflicts of taste, it engages in more retroactive rationalization than convincing illumination—and its verdicts on "good taste" often conveniently align with the taste the writer happens to hold.

In one landmark essay, "Of the Standard of Taste" (1757), David Hume describes the tasteful person in terms that seem intuitively right: "Strong sense, united to delicate sentiment, improved by practice, perfected by comparison and cleared of all prejudice, can alone entitle critics to this valuable character; and the joint verdict of such, wherever they are to be found, is the true standard of taste and beauty." But that's a job description for critics, not a standard of taste. For that, Hume can only appeal to authority: the tasteful person will give approbation to works that stand the test of time—the works still approved by tasteful people later. It's a tautological, survival-of-the-fittest view that's no help in resolving quarrels of taste in our own lifetimes. His stipulation that the critic be credentialed with wide knowledge and experience could itself be described as a prejudice—a bias in favor of tradition, which may punish deviation from the "highest" standards and obstruct the creation of new ones. Exactly this kind of prejudice kept most high-culture Brahmins from accepting pop music or film as art at all until the 1960s. Hume acknowledges the need for artistic change, but he underestimates how determinedly his elite of taste aristocrats would resist it: the demand to be at once expert and unbiased is enough of a paradox that you could say Hume's ideal critic by definition cannot exist.

Aesthetic philosophy's other great-granddaddy is Immanuel Kant. His Third Critique, *The Critique of Judgment* (1790), like Hume's essay, begins from the dilemma that people can disagree on what is beautiful. But the parts of the Third Critique that dazzle are its limnings of the nature of beauty and of the sublime, and its subtly kinetic account of how reason, imagination and perception interact in "free play" to produce aesthetic judgment: Kant seems almost to intuit, two centuries in advance, how disparate chambers of the brain light up simultaneously when we listen to music, as recounted in Levitin's book. When he tries to account for how these processes produce opposing judgments, however, Kant falls back on a fantasy that there's a *sensus communis,* a "common sense" of beauty that *would* generate a consensus if only there were "ideal" conditions—including ample education, leisure, etcetera. Aesthetic agreement only eludes us because circumstances distort some people's perceptions. A modern reader can't help noticing that Kant's ideal conditions suspiciously resemble being an educated eighteenth-century gentleman in cultured Koenigsburg. This "common sense" is not only unconvincing from a contemporary, diversity-oriented viewpoint—it doesn't even sound *desirable*.

But some of his insights still seem crucial. Kant was the first to say that aesthetic judgments are by nature unprovable—they can't be reduced to logic. Nevertheless, he pointed out, they always feel necessary and universal: when we think something's great, we want everyone else to think it's great too.

Not long after Kant and Hume, whose contributions were only the weightiest in a more widespread dispute, the veracity of taste was largely put on the philosophical shelf. The "man of taste" tended to become a caricature—a figure out of Molière or Oscar Wilde, the dandy who lavishes more care on niceties of form and style than on deeper values. (In fact the clinching portrait of such a character was drawn even in the thick of the Enlightenment, in Denis Diderot's extraordinary *Rameau's Nephew*.) Many writers (Nietzsche among them) have lambasted Kant, in particular, for saying the appreciator of beauty must be "disinterested," adopting a personal distance from the origins, content and implications—the meaning, if you will—of the work of art.

The great American art critic Clement Greenberg, one of the rare later thinkers to take up the question, suggested that Romantic ideology raised art to such a sacred status in the nineteenth century that it seemed gauche to call attention to the process of evaluating it. Following Kant, Greenberg offered brilliant descriptions of the mental "switch" that is flipped when we regard something aesthetically—as we can do with anything, he argued, not just art, by contemplating an object or scene or person as "an end in itself," apart from any other role or use—echoing Kant's definition of beauty as "purposiveness without purpose." Greenberg was also lucid on Kant's insinuation that to enjoy art is also to judge it—you like it because it gives pleasure, but it can't give you pleasure if you don't like it.

Greenberg's answer to taste conflict, however, was the same as Hume's: we know there is objective taste because, over time, a consensus is reached on the great works of the past. (Never mind that anything ruled out by previous generations' consensus is probably lost and unlikely to come messing with the current consensus.) The most objective taste in the present, he said, belongs to those who know that canon deeply but are also open to novelty. Which (surprise, surprise) sounds a lot like Clement Greenberg, although his openness seemed to ebb by the mid-1960s, when he began trashing new art movements as a decline from the modernism on which he'd made his critical reputation—a vivid case of the contradiction between mandarinism and flexibility. And that's not even to mention his dismissal of mass culture as, first, "kitsch" and, later, "middlebrow"—either way, the enemy of "genuine" culture.

Rather than by science or philosophy, the story of how aesthetic judgment reached the crisis felt by Komar and Melamid is best understood as a product of western art itself. To oversimplify wantonly, the disenchantment begins with the severing of visual art and music in particular from their religious role, in which the Church (and, rhetorically, God) is the ultimate art critic. After the Enlightenment, art gradually moves from an aristocratic status to a bourgeois one. The Romantics, in reaction, celebrate artistic genius as an autonomous agent of revelation, proudly outside society. Modernism gives that outsider status a harder edge: Art's mission becomes not just to reveal higher truth but also to attack social falsehood. The very idea of "beauty" becomes a second-rate capitulation to bourgeois values—now ugliness, obscenity, formlessness and randomness all can be in the best of taste. Innovation becomes the yardstick, as artists continually attempt to outpace taste, to violate its terms or render it irrelevant. The belief is that to bring about a higher consciousness, it's necessary not just to delight with newness but also to mount a shock attack on the old, bourgeois, decadent consciousness. As critic Boris Groys puts it, "Now it is not the observer who judges the artwork, but the artwork that judges—and often condemns—its public." The motivations are varied—for some, it's a psychoanalysis-inspired faith in the irrational; for others, it is revolutionary politics or plain misanthropy; for most, it's just what bohemians do. And improbably, they succeed. Not that taste comes to an end, but the expectation of consensus withers.

This is possible because attacks on conventional taste have been mounted from several directions. It's an outcome of the disillusioning course of the twentieth century, as sounded in Theodor Adorno's question of how to write poetry after Auschwitz. But mainly it's a more upbeat, good-humored attack from the paradoxical partnership of capitalism—which seeks to remove any barriers to reaching all possible marketplaces—and democracy, which fosters the view that elite opinion is no better than anyone else's. (Today they've been supplemented by their advanced outgrowths, globalization and identity politics.) The most powerful vehicle for that alliance is mass culture. Pop songs and movies and genre fiction and magazines are so appealing, achieve so much aesthetically for so many people, that snobbery cannot hold the line against them. With Pop Art, camp aesthetics and rock'n'roll, the notions of highbrow, middlebrow and lowbrow—which from nearly the dawn of mass culture dominated discussions of taste (see historian Michael Kammen's *American Culture, American Tastes*)—start to fall apart. By the early twenty-first century, almost no one believes in them.

Among artists themselves, the continual process of violating limits seems to reach an endpoint or at least exhaustion, and anything-goes eclecticism takes its place (critic and philosopher Arthur Danto calls this "the end of art history" or "post-art"). Among audiences, a growing fragmentation and subculturization accomplishes similar ends: though indie-rock and classical listeners, science-fiction fans and architecture buffs, rockabillies and swing kids, hip-hop heads and salsa dancers may believe strongly in their own tastes, in aggregate they are acclimatized to the notion that separate "taste worlds" can coexist peacefully, without need for external, official inspection and verification.

Early on, this shift brought pop-culture criticism into its own. While there had been a few serious commentators on movies and jazz, the treatment of pop and mass culture in North America was mainly confined to light journalism until the advent of writers such as Pauline Kael and Andrew Sarris on film (as well as their equivalents in France) and the "counterculture" press that created rock criticism, with writers such as Robert Christgau, Greil Marcus, Lester Bangs and Ellen Willis. While film critics usually made the case that film deserved appreciation on a par with high art, rock criticism began with a more radical stance against elite taste, arguing *no* work was too humble for aesthetic contemplation—that a form's most "low" or "impure" qualities could be its strengths. As the field grew, that attitude was watered down: some writers reintroduced traditional hierarchies in updated forms; a rough idea of a pop/rock canon began to coalesce in books like the *Rolling Stone Record Guides*; other fans and critics, especially after punk, adopted a harsh line on "selling out" to an entertainment industry that, like Greenberg or Adorno before them, they considered a capitalist scheme to foist brainless product on a beclouded public; and so on. The debates over "rockism" and "popism" are symptoms of present unease about standards and subjectivism, as is, of course, this book. But the mandate to dethrone taste orthodoxies remains part of pop criticism's legacy, so much so that it may help bring its own extinction: Within what more than one writer has called "No-Brow" culture, who needs professional critics? What do they offer, if not objectivity?

The one bothersome matter in this anarchic taste universe (a utopia or dystopia, depending on your ideology, but one that cannot be wished away) is the persistence of a mainstream—what Greenberg or his contemporary Dwight Macdonald would have called "middlebrow" culture, the politely domineering realm where Céline Dion is queen, unattached to any validating subculture. Middlebrow is the new lowbrow—mainstream taste the only taste for which you still have to say you're sorry. And there, taste seems less an aesthetic question than, again, a social one: among the thousands of varieties of aesthetes and geeks and hobbyists, each with their special-ordered cultural diet, the abiding mystery of mainstream culture is, "Who the hell *are* those people?" Perhaps Komar and Melamid are right: the way to the heart of taste today may be through a poll.

8.
Let's Talk About
Who's Got Bad Taste

The poll I have in mind was conducted in the mid-1960s in France by a team of researchers under sociologist Pierre Bourdieu. It surveyed thousands of people on what kinds of culture they knew, liked and participated in—not just in the arts, but sports, hobbies, foods, styles of dress and furniture, the newspapers and TV programs they followed, etcetera. All this data was correlated with information about their incomes, education levels, family backgrounds and occupations, and supplemented with interviews in which people were asked to discuss and defend their preferences.

The result was a milestone of social science, Bourdieu's 1979 tome *Distinction: A Social Critique of the Judgement of Taste*. Note the subtitle, a flip of the bird to Kant's Enlightenment notion of disinterested aesthetic judgment: For Bourdieu, taste is always interested—in fact, self-interested—and those interests are *social*. His theories press the point that aesthetics are social all the way down, just a set of euphemisms for a starker system of inequality and competition: if you flinch at seeing a copy of *Let's Talk About Love* or *The DaVinci Code* on a friend's shelves, what you are trying to shake off is the stain of the déclassé, the threat of social inferiority.

What made him think so? His survey data had confirmed stereotypes to a staggering degree: almost exclusively, French people with working-class jobs knew and liked only relatively "lowbrow" culture; the middle classes liked "middlebrow" stuff; and the better-off were patrons of "highbrow" culture. Aesthetic and lifestyle choices even clustered along more minute divisions within classes: workers in factories had different tastes than workers in shopping centers; office managers differed from small-business owners; surgeons' tastes were unlike those of corporate executives.

But it was in asking people the reasons behind their choices that Bourdieu exploded the assumptions embedded in the whole "brow" system (which originated in racist nineteenth-century theories about facial features and intelligence). What he found was that poorer people were pragmatic about their tastes, describing them as entertaining, useful and accessible. But from the middle classes up, people had much grander justifications. For one thing, they were far more confident about their dislikes, about what was tacky or lame. But they also spoke in elaborate detail about how their tastes reflected their values and personalities, and in what areas they still wanted to enrich their knowledge.

Bourdieu's interpretation was that tastes were serving as strategic tools. While working-class tastes seemed mainly a default (serving at best to express group belongingness and solidarity), for everyone else taste was not only a product of economic and educational background but, as it developed through life, a force mobilized as part of their quest for social status (or what Bourdieu called symbolic power). What we have agreed to call tastes, he said, is an array of symbolic associations we use to set ourselves apart from those whose social ranking is beneath us, and to take aim at the status we think we deserve. Taste is a means of distinguishing ourselves from others, the pursuit of *distinction.* And its end product is to perpetuate and reproduce the class structure.

His argument may seem less counterintuitive if you put it in terms of evolutionary psychology: if human beings are driven to advance in status in order to acquire mates and provide security to their offspring, Bourdieu was proposing that taste is a tool of those instincts, used to gain competitive advantage; and in a capitalist society, class is how this competition is structured (and exacerbated), to the advantage of the dominant elite.

Was he saying that when you become a bank manager, you automatically start liking the music other bank managers like? No, nothing so mechanical. Unlike previous, reductive Marxist theorists of culture, Bourdieu wanted to account for the fact that we experience tastes as both spontaneous attractions and personal choices. To square individuality and agency with the consistency of his data, he needed new conceptual terms. He made an analogy with economics: Imagine that capital comes in forms other than money and property, such as *cultural capital* (knowledge and experience of culture, ideas and references) and *social capital* (personal connections and influence), terms he coined that have come into common usage. As with money, cultural and social capital's value depends on scarcity, on knowing what others don't. Sometimes forms of capital are interchangeable: I can buy cultural knowledge through education, which may lead to a better job and con-

CARL WILSON

nections. Often they are not: a university professor may have top-flight cultural and social capital, but she cannot command a CEO's salary. For Bourdieu, class is determined not just by income or occupation but by how much of all these forms of capital you have, and in what combinations.

The class segment you're born, raised and schooled in produces what Bourdieu called your *habitus*, meaning both your *home base* and your *habits*: the attitudes, abilities and expectations your upbringing has nurtured. You then make choices, consciously or unconsciously, to maximize your satisfaction in life within the bounds your *habitus* makes thinkable: it does not dictate what you do, but it serves as a filter for your predilections and decisions. It's like a jazz musician improvising on a standard: You can alter the notes and rhythms of the melody, but your improvisation is limited by the tempo and chord changes available in the song. To choose otherwise would be to play "badly" and discordantly and risk failure and ostracization. (On the Bourdieuvian bandstand, there is no free jazz.)

Along with *habitus*, the other major social structures for Bourdieu are *fields*—social institutions or networks through which we pursue our goals, such as the political, cultural, corporate, academic, legal, medical or religious fields (each including subfields with their own rules and pecking orders). The pursuit of distinction takes place in those fields. Tastes are the result of the interaction of *habitus* and field—attempts, informed by our backgrounds, to advance our status by accumulating cultural and social capital in particular spheres—and, perhaps more importantly, to prevent ourselves from ever being mistaken for someone of a lower status. Bourdieu wrote that "tastes are perhaps first and foremost distastes, disgusts provoked by horror or visceral intolerance of the tastes of others."

His point is not that people are only pretending to like or dislike the culture they like and dislike, trying to con people into thinking highly of them. The pleasure of listening to music or playing a sport is obviously real. The argument is that the *kinds* of music and sports we choose, and how we talk about them, are socially shaped—that the cultural filters and concepts that guide my interests in and reactions to music, clothes, films or home decoration come out of my class and field. At worst I am conning myself, but to what I feel is my advantage.

It's not so strange an idea that there are social subtexts to our tastes: You might be a Julliard music student with a trust fund who associates authenticity with the inner city or the backwoods, and feel a little realer yourself when you kick it to Snoop or clean the condo with some bluegrass on. You may be less enamored of what you imagine about frat boys or soccer moms, and avoid music that conjures up such listeners. Or if you *are* a soccer mom, you may want to be the soccer mom who listens to Slayer, because you want to stay a little young and wild, not like those soccer moms who listen to Sheryl Crow.

In early twenty-first-century terms, for most people under fifty, distinction boils down to *cool*. Cool confers status—symbolic power. It incorporates both cultural capital and social capital, and it's a clear potential route to economic capital. Corporations and culture-makers pursue it as much as individuals do. It changes attributes in different milieus. As much as we avow otherwise, few of us are truly indifferent to cool, not a little anxious about whether we have enough, and Bourdieu's theory may illustrate why that's not merely shallow: Being uncool has material consequences. Sexual opportunity, career advancement and respect, even elementary security can ride on it. To ignore cool may mean risking downward mobility at a time when many people are falling out of the middle class.

Even being *deliberately* uncool doesn't save you, as that's an attempt to flip the rules in your favor. Having a "guilty pleasure," for instance, can be an asset in this system of cultural capital because it suggests that you are so cool that you can afford to risk it on something goofy, ungainly and awkward—which makes you that much cooler. A few people with real panache, like an Andy Warhol or John Waters, can assemble taste profiles that consist of nothing *but* guilty pleasures and be ultra-cool, but that takes at least social capital, so that the kitsch connoisseur can be distinguished from the doofus who just likes goofball stuff. (For you to be cool requires someone else to be less cool.)

The clearest way to understand distinction may be in high-school terms: Say you're a white, nerdy fifteen-year-old boy who listens to *High School Musical* (if you're too old to know what *High School Musical* is, substitute the Andrew Lloyd Webber of your choice) but you come to see you have a chance at becoming friends with the tough kids who smoke behind the school. So you start listening to death metal and wearing hacked-up jean jackets. This isn't a ruse: you just start to see what's *plausible* and *exciting* for you about those tastes. Here, death metal is cultural capital, high-school cliques are the field and your *habitus* is what's likely to determine whether you can carry off the slang and the haircut. Your instinct is to distinguish yourself from the nerds by becoming one of the tough kids, who, incidentally, hate *High*

School Musical (or *Cats*) with a vengeance, because that's what nerds listen to. That's distinction.

The indie-rock cliché of "I *used* to like that band"—i.e., until people like *you* liked them—is a sterling example of distinction in action. In fact, distinction helps explain the rapidity of artistic change (artists are competing for distinction) as well as some of the resistance: changing styles threaten to bankrupt some people's cultural capital, to lower the status of those who associated themselves with the older style. Bourdieu argues innovation will usually come from individuals in a field who do not yet have secure positions, attempting to change the game to their own advantage, while established artists, curators, critics, producers, etcetera, try for as long as they can to preserve the rules by which they were winning.

Distinction might also demystify Kant's claim that taste always desires others' agreement. Your love of hip-hop or hatred for Céline Dion (or vice-versa) is part of your cultural capital, but it only gains value in the competition for distinction if it is *legitimated* in the contexts that matter to you. Unlike Kant, though, Bourdieu would say the last thing you want is that agreement be universal: you want your taste affirmed by your peers and those you admire, but it's just as vital that your redneck uncle thinks you're an idiot to like that rap shit. It proves you've distinguished yourself from him successfully, and can bask in righteous satisfaction.

To the extent we agree that coolness and lack of same are enormously influential—and that coolness is a social category, not a natural attribute (with the possible exception of Keith Richards)—we are all Bourdieuvians.

* * *

One of Bourdieu's most striking notions is that there's also an inherent antagonism between people in fields structured mainly by cultural capital and those in fields where there is primarily economic capital: while high-ranking artists and intellectuals are part of the dominant class in society thanks to their education and influence, they are a *dominated* segment of that class compared to actual *rich* people. This helps explain why so many artists, journalists and academics can see themselves as anti-establishment subversives while most of the public sees them as smug elitists. And this opposition between cultural and economic capital carries down into less-privileged class strata, perhaps helping to motivate school teachers to vote for Democrats (currently the party associated with cultural capital) and auto workers to vote Republican (symbolically the party of economic capital).

Artistic taste is most competitive among people whose main asset is cultural capital. That's why high school serves as such a vivid backdrop for illustrations of how distinction in artistic taste works: Not only is high school a field we all know, it's one in which there's practically nothing but cultural and social capital; money plays more of a backstage role. In adult life, it's only in culture-centered fields (the arts, academia) that musical or other artistic taste matters the way it does in high school. However, recall that Bourdieu defines taste very broadly, to include tastes in clothes, food, leisure activities, architecture and interior decoration, sports, news sources, etcetera, and you can see how much taste continues to count for the social position of adults in business and political life.

The theory of distinction is reminiscent of Thorstein Veblen's famous critique of conspicuous consumption, but it is less liable to self-congratulatory misreading. It's not that some people are in the grip of a craven obsession with keeping up the Joneses while less materialistic sorts can stand aloof. *Inconspicuous* consumption can be distinction-oriented too: It distinguishes us from those tacky, materialist people. No one is exempt.

And neither is any artistic field. Bourdieu's tools also offer a revision of the mid-century Frankfurt School critique of the Culture Industry, in which Theodor Adorno and Max Horkheimer (having witnessed the Nazi use of mass communications for propaganda) talked about popular culture as if it were a quasi-fascist conspiracy to dull and numb the masses. What if, instead, the mass-cultural field is just another zone of competition for distinction, no more or less venal than others? Bourdieu (who died in 2002 at age seventy-one) disliked mass culture himself, but his theories imply that high culture is at least as culpable for social inequity as popular culture is, riddled with gambits to raise its own status and derogate its inferiors. By Bourdieu's lights, if there's such a thing as false consciousness, then everybody has it, at least until they become self-conscious of the social nature of their tastes. It's a useful corrective to the biases of fans and critics who think alternative or independent music is somehow inherently less status-seeking, more real, than pop music. (Which is simply a less-coherent repeat of Adorno's anticommercial attack on jazz.)

The translation of *distinction* to *cool* leads us to one of the problems with applying Bourdieu's model nearly forty years after his research: his original survey did not reflect the relatively recent shakeup in taste categories, the seeming collapse of high and low culture into a No-Brow society in which an in-depth knowledge of *Buffy the Vampire Slayer*, Japanese *ganguro* fashions and the latest graffiti artists may carry more cachet than a conversance with Molière, Schoenberg and Donald Judd. Does that mean his theory is outmoded?

No. For Bourdieu, it doesn't matter what the objects of good taste are at any moment. Change the value of x and the equation stays the same. He notes that a once-refined or highbrow piece of music, such as the *Moonlight Sonata*, can be reassigned to middlebrow culture when it has become overly familiar. Its relative uncoolness is an attribute not of the composition, but of its commonplaceness. Cool things gradually become uncool.

Still, in a hyper-mediated, mass-production culture, a lot of reference points are shared across classes. Almost everyone now will wear jeans. Nearly everybody has spent time listening to rock music. So there is more mixing and matching than Bourdieu's theories would seem to permit. American sociologists Richard Petersen and Roger Kern in the mid-1990s suggested that the upper-class taste model had changed from a "snob" to an "omnivore" ideal, in which the coolest thing for a well-off and well-educated person to do is to consume some high culture *along* with heaps of popular culture, international art and lowbrow entertainment: a contemporary opera one evening, the roller derby and an Afrobeat show the next. They speculate that the shift corresponds to a new elite requirement to be able to "code switch" in varied cultural settings, due to multiculturalism and globalization. (Bourdieu's own son Emmanuel, now a film director in his forties, is a perfect omnivore, according to a recent profile in *The New York Times*: "He's capable of speaking equally seriously about Leibniz's philosophy and about Antonio Banderas's *Legend of Zorro*.") Petersen and Kern thought it likely that the less privileged would, correspondingly, have narrower patterns of cultural consumption; other researchers think there might be distinct upper-, middle- and lower-class omnivore styles.

But nobody is a true omnivore. To have taste at all means to exclude. It's one thing to prove that well-off people now listen to classical *and* rock *and* hip-hop, read literary novels *and* watch sitcoms, but to show there aren't subtler hierarchies of preference would require dauntingly in-depth research. Most available studies suffer from an inbuilt bias: academics, as the studies themselves show, are nearly the only group in con-temporary society that still pays most of its attention to high culture. So when they design their surveys, they ask people to choose between Bach, Philip Glass and hip-hop, not between, say, pop-chart hip-hop, cocaine-rap mixtapes and politicized underground rap, even though each one carries status and identity implications. Distinctions in a culture that valorizes omnivorism are simply that much more fine-grained, fast-changing and invidious.

Even without more meticulous divisions, though, you can still detect class bias in omnivore tastes: In a paper titled "'Anything But Heavy Metal': Symbolic Exclusion and Musical Dislikes," Princeton sociologist Bethany Bryson compiled data on musical tastes and political attitudes, by education level, from the 1993 General Social Survey (conducted annually by a research center at the University of Chicago). Sure enough, she found that the most educated, high-cultural-capital respon-dents (who were also the most politically liberal and racially tol-erant) disliked the fewest forms of music. In particular, highly educated white people were much less likely to reject Latin, jazz, blues and R&B than other white respondents; Bryson described them as maximizing their "multicultural capital." But they did have music they disliked—the four types that had the *least-educated* fans: rap, heavy metal, country and gospel. Since in 1993 anti-rap feelings cut across all groups, in fact the white omnivores were distinguishing themselves quite specifically from "white trash." (Is this perhaps a reason Céline is more swiftly and rudely ejected from music discussions than her black-diva counterparts?)

As well, even when they're enjoying the same stuff, the classes still have different motivations. In a study in the *Journal of Consumer Research* in 1998, sociologist Douglas B. Holt found that there was plenty of high-and-low cultural mixology going on among the people he interviewed in a small Pennsylvania town, especially among higher-status subjects. But the "low cultural capital" interviewees talked about their cultural choices as practical, fun, community-oriented and easy to relate to. Meanwhile the "high cultural capital" subjects described their preferences as showing authenticity, uniqueness, quality, cosmopolitanism and personal creative expression. Overall, to quote the Starkist tuna ad, lower-class respondents said what they liked "tasted good," while the higher-class ones said what they liked was "in good taste." Just as in France in the mid-sixties, the privileged felt their tastes set them apart from the common horde and made them special.

* * *

At this point I should say that I don't think Bourdieu was entirely right.

Recent studies indicate that while social status—income and education—does correlate significantly with tastes and distastes, it is not nearly as all-explanatory as it seemed in Bourdieu's study. Other factors turn out to play a comparable role, such as ethnicity, gender and regional background. Other times tastes don't fall into any sociologically measurable categories. Perhaps France in the 1960s was unusually rigid and orthodox in its class stratifications (although in North America, class-mobility data says the average person is much less likely to rise in status today compared to thirty years ago). More likely, his research was unconsciously designed to present the strongest case for what he already believed, as research so often is: you might say Bourdieu's taste in survey questions operated to increase his own cultural capital. More generously, he was overcorrecting against the insular, ivory-tower view of taste and aesthetic "disinterestedness" that had come down from Kant through the cultural elite for two centuries, and shouting to make his point heard.

On top of that, his tendency to blame everything unpleasant about the way taste functions on modern capitalism was, well, very French. I suspect that the status-seeking reflex he was describing would re-emerge in any complex society: it can be ameliorated but not eliminated. Besides, we didn't start loving beauty, enjoying songs, making pictures and discussing them solely for competitive advantage. While they may be shaped partly to that end, we also do them for their own sake, for all the benefits traditionally ascribed to artistic experience. But even if Bourdieu was only fifty percent right—if taste is only *half* a subconscious mechanism by which we fight for power and status, mainly by condemning people we consider "beneath" us—that would be twice as complicit in class discrimination as most of us would like to think our aesthetics are.

And his account does feel at least half-accurate as a description of what is happening when I react allergically to Céline Dion. I'm intuiting that there's no sleight of hand or subtle reinterpretation I can use to fit her music into my store of cultural capital: it can only make me dorkier if I listen to it, so I push it away hard and fast. Conversely, her fans, from another class or field standpoint, find something in the music that seems to increase their own cultural capital, the value of her voice or her romanticism or her westernness, so they latch on.

Besides being a bright caution light against rushing to call musicians naff, tacky or *kétaine*, this thought is discouraging for our experiment: Even if I can set my prejudices and status anxieties aside in a more fundamental way than Hume ever imagined, and find aspects of Céline's music to embrace, the research suggests that I'm not going to appreciate her in the same terms her fans do. The very act of writing this book suggests an effort to plug her back into my pre-existing, class-based sets of culture processors . . . perhaps by granting her a role in a social critique. Indeed you could fairly say that my experiment is an attempt to expand my cultural capital among music critics, to gain symbolic status by being the most omnivorous of all. My only answer is that any move I make as a critic is open to similar charges. What can you do? The game of distinction may reproduce class structure, but it also makes the world go 'round.

Still, that all depends whether Céline fans and I really, as Bourdieu would predict, come from different walks of life, at least enough so that I would want to distinguish myself from their "bad taste." That jerk in the *Independent* who said that Céline's fan base must be in "some middle-of-the-road Middle England invisible to the rest of us" was indulging in a bit of speculative Bourdieuvian sociology, extrapolating from taste to characterize her devotees as "grannies, tux-wearers, overweight children, mobile-phone salesmen," images straight out of the BBC's class-hatred comedy series, *Little Britain*. I'd prefer something a bit more empirical, but I don't have a team of researchers to phone up thousands of households. Luckily, Céline's record company does.

* * *

The NPD Group, a market-research company in New York, assembled a demographic profile of American Céline Dion consumers for Sony from January of 2005 to December of 2006. It doesn't tell us whether they are overweight or sell mobile phones but what it does say is suggestive. It compared Céline listeners to US music consumers as a whole: In age, for example, the Céline Dion buyer was 75 percent less likely than your average music buyer to be a teenager. Aside from a bump in the early twenties (perhaps because those people were teens when *Titanic* and *Let's Talk About Love* came out), her audience skews to the over-thirty-five—in fact, around 45 percent of Céline listeners were over fifty, compared to only 20 percent of music buyers overall. Add to that the fact that 68 percent of her listeners were female: Grannies? Check. In fact, Céline fans were about three-and-a-half times more likely to be *widowed* than the average music listener. It's hard to imagine an audience that could confer less cool on a musician.

Céline fans were less likely than the average music buyer to be black, though 13 percent of them were. Reflecting her global-star status, they were more likely than most music fans to be neither black nor white. They were less likely to live on the coasts than in the "red" or "fly-over" states, the US equivalent of "Middle England," plus that haven for older ladies, Florida. They tended to buy their Céline albums from big-box discount stores, and often they discovered her on TV. They were *much* less likely than other consumers to be downloading songs on the Internet, legally or illegally.

But let's get to the meatier socioeconomics: A disproportionate part of her audience was in the lowest income bracket, under $25,000 a year, and again in the next-lowest category. Her fans were relatively underrepresented in the high-income brackets (over $75,000 a year), but a quarter of them did claim to make at least that much. It was education that gave me a surprise: Céline fans were significantly *less* likely than the average music buyer to have only a high-school education or less. The shortage of teenagers helps explain that, but not entirely. More often, they had "some college," meaning an incomplete degree (or perhaps a community-college certificate), but the number of college graduates was only slightly below average, and those with "post-college" schooling slightly above (which could mean grad school but could also mean continuing education).

It's vague, but it does stimulate the imagination. Rather than the abject losers of the *Independent*'s fantasy, what I picture is a striving bunch (grannies included), many of them with training in what I would guess (combining the education and income stats) are the ill-paid "helping professions," such as nursing, teaching, public relations, human resources and other middle-class service careers. Bourdieu painted these people (with far less sympathy than he had for manual workers and petty clerks) as the ultimate middlebrow sector, "the new petite bourgeois," who he said demonstrated an excess of "cultural goodwill": Having disconnected from their likely roots in working-class culture, they were gamely but not very suavely trying to adjust themselves to what they believed were "the higher things." In his interviews he found that they held a fairly straightlaced set of moral values, tempered by a sentimental streak. Full of aspiration, but with prospects much lower than their dreams, they might fairly be guessed to overlap with readers of self-help books and attendees of motivational seminars. And based on their low Internet usage, not to mention the retro character of Céline's schmaltz, there probably aren't a lot of bloggers and tech heads. In the wealthier part of the listenership, you'd probably find much of the Vegas crowd—middle managers, lower-rung executives and their families (or their widows), with a sizable smattering of business immigrants and ESL students. The survey didn't ask about sexual orientation, but with diva audiences, and Céline's in particular, there's little doubt gay men and lesbians are also represented, possibly skewing up the income and education curves.

Widows and grannies aside, what occurs to me is that this midlevel cultural-capital audience is not as far from the average white pop critic as we might have expected. We usually make middling incomes or worse, and while most have university degrees, our expertise is usually more self-taught than PhD-certified, a pattern Bourdieu believed would produce an anxious, fact-hoarding intellectual style in contrast with the relaxed mastery of a fully legitimated cultural elite. (If you've met any pop critics, you'll see his point.) When a critic or heavily invested music buff says, as they often do, that discovering music or writing "saved my life," I think what lurks behind the melodrama is a feeling that a facility with pop culture and words has saved us *from* the life of subservient career, suburban lifestyle and quiet desperation we imagine befalls people like Céline Dion's white American fans, as well as fans of Billy Joel, Michael Bolton and the other midlevel musicians whose names so often serve us as epithets. Perhaps our scathing tongues are enacting what Freud called the narcissism of small differences, in defense of what Bourdieu might call a very fragile distinction. If middlebrow has been designated the new lowbrow, maybe this is why.

Enough surveys, then. It's time to go out and meet some Céline fans. At least to say I'm sorry.

9.
Let's Talk with Some Fans

It seemed like a good idea at the time: if you want to find Céline Dion fans, go to Las Vegas, to her nightly extravaganza *A New Day*. I would ask who they were, why they came, how they felt about the star's mixed reputation. What I hadn't counted on was Vegas. It was my first visit. I stupidly came alone. If there is a laboratory demonstration of the antagonism between economic and cultural capital, it is Las Vegas, a city of such pure commercialism that money is its entertainment, interrupted occasionally by a show. Nowhere else is it so palpable that art can be simply the green kid stepping in to give a brief break to the main, fiduciary attraction. Alcohol and sex, too, are reduced to lubricants for or aftereffects of finance. In this nonstop carnival of social inversion, only money is purely beautiful, in Kant's sense of being an end in itself. Vegas's fabled love of the ersatz, like its mini Eiffel Tower, is money giddily blaspheming culture's sacred icons. All of which, in the abstract, seems kind of healthy. But in the flesh it depressed the hell out of me. I am averse to gambling. I am entirely too shy to hire prostitutes. In Sin City that leaves a solitary man at loose ends. I wandered in a haze through the gold towers and black pyramids, dancing water fountains, seizure-inducing signage and replicas of landmarks from cities where I'd rather have been, before slouching back to my room each night with a fifth of bourbon to watch pay-per-view. Muttering witticisms to myself got tired fast. I was a stray member of the cultural-capital tribe deported to a gaudy prison colony run by a phalanx of showgirls who held hourly re-education sessions to hammer me into feeling insignificant and micro-penised.

In my shriveled condition, the notion of interviewing people at Caesar's seemed as absurd as some peasant dropping in on Versailles in the 1680s to demand the courtiers' opinions of Louis XIV. If I'd had better props than my tiny voice recorder, ideally a TV crew, I might have mustered the nerve to interrupt people's holidays with my fruity questions. But now I would have to find another way. Like any journalist caught in a cul de sac, I turned to the Internet.

* * *

The furthest-out Céline website has to be CelineDreams. com, a forum created in 2001 by portrait photographer Yuri Toroptsov, who grew up in a 300-person Russian farming village, became a Céline fan on a business trip to South Korea and discovered dream interpretation in a Psych class in New York. His readers submit dreams they've had featuring Céline, and Toroptsov replies with affable armchair analysis. Here's dream No. 67, from twenty-year-old Bella in the UK: "In my dream I was 13. I flew out to the USA alone and arrived at her house with the adoption papers ready for her to sign. When I got there, Céline wasn't in, I started to panic, I only had a one-way ticket. The maid who answered the door only spoke French and I couldn't understand what she was saying. Just as the maid was about to close the door, I heard a car coming up the drive, it was Céline. She got out and I handed her the papers, she thought I was just another fan wanting her autograph so she signed. I explained that they were adoption papers, she smiled and took my hand. Then I woke up."

Toroptsov generously overlooks Bella's commission of adoption fraud. Instead, he counsels, "It looks like that you are looking for some external support. In your dream Céline symbolizes that kind of ideal caretaker. She is well-known, famous and understanding. The French-speaking maid stands for the obstacles and fears you meet on your way."

Céline as substitute mom or caring confidante turns up a lot in the dreams, from fans ranging from ten to their mid-fifties. Most are celebrity-wish-fulfillment (often including a vocal duet), a few are romances, and several are nightmares of Céline losing her voice. But then there's the one in which Céline is *ironing live snakes* in a fan's living room, or the person who dreams Céline has stolen his magic flying helmet. She forcibly washes another dreamer's face using a wet, live kitten. (I know the feeling from her records.) In an interview with Yahoo.com, Toroptsov admitted he has to filter out a lot of less-benign submissions: "I think 'laughing at me' is actually a real driver of traffic to my site." But he thinks that's "healthy."

That easygoingness is common in Céline's Internet world, much more than on the message boards I'm accustomed to. Like any fans, they trade news and clips, debate import remixes, compare their heroine to other divas. Surf-by "Céline sucks" attacks are taken in stride. The most heated battles I read were over whether Madonna and Mariah are talented in their own ways or just crazy sluts. There is just the tiniest bit of Céline porn. I posted a call for interview subjects, knowing I was skewing my sample, since the typical Céline fan is not that plugged-in: nobody who got in touch was a widow; the few older respondents kept missing my phone calls. But I did chat with six or seven younger fans in Canada, the US, Britain and Brazil. Here are a few highlights.

* * *

Joe Nielsen, who lives in Sonoma County, California, about ninety minutes north of San Francisco, is the most over-the-top Céline fanatic I meet. He has seen her live "about twelve" times and has a substantial Céline collection. He writes songs influenced by her style, and has finagled his way backstage in Vegas to submit some staging ideas that he thinks may have been incorporated, rejigged, into *A New Day*. "One of the higher-ups" at his work, the credit office of a home-improvement store, teases him by calling him "Céline."

Joe also has his reasons. Unlike just about anyone in North America, Joe first heard "My Heart Will Go On" on the Internet. "It was being played on all the radio stations, of course," he says. "But I was going through a rough time and I wasn't paying attention to much." He was fifteen or sixteen. His mother was an alcoholic, and his father was in the Merchant Marines and mostly off at sea. Joe was also realizing he was gay. "I started contemplating some form of suicide. . . . I didn't feel like anyone would notice." When he downloaded "My Heart

Will Go On," it "helped draw me out of darkness and into the light. . . . I realized through that song that the reason I am put here on Earth is to help people through hard times, or happy times. Without it, I don't know if I'd be here today."

It is impossible not to identify with the archetypal narrative Joe's story presents: in your darkest moment, you hear a song or read a book that lets you know you aren't alone. It may be the most intense sort of artistic encounter we ever have. But usually the musician is someone like Kurt Cobain, the novel something like *Catcher in the Rye*. When the talisman turns out to be something thought so trite as "My Heart Will Go On," the empathy can shift to doubting the subject's mental fitness. Yet Joe is quite articulate and reflective in his fandom: He feels Céline's French material "seems to have a deeper soul or meaning to it" (he doesn't speak French but would like to learn) and "a lot of the English material, as much as I love it, can be . . . like it's what everybody else is doing." He's partial to her dance music, and collects DJ remixes, thinking Céline would get less flack from non-fans if they knew she's not just a "ballad queen."

Joe dropped out of high school in twelfth grade but he recently got his GED. Now twenty-three, when we spoke he was working out and trying to lose weight, and had moved back in with his dad to save up money to get a place with Raymond, his boyfriend. Raymond wasn't a Céline fan when they met. "It's definitely interesting to have friends who don't really like the artists a person likes—the world's all about diversity," Joe says. But he's also made friends through the Céline message boards, traveling with them to Vegas. He listens to Gloria Estefan and Britney Spears, but also to country, "and I do like Frank Sinatra as well." But he mainly dreams of meeting Céline, "just to say 'thank you for inspiring me every day' and making me a better human being—and it'd be great to have her sing one or two of my songs. Who knows?"

* * *

Stockton, California's Sophoan Sorn is another fan in his early twenties who imagines collaborating someday with Céline—it must be a California thing. His chances seem a bit better, though: he's a full-time film production student in San Francisco, and has run his own photography and documentary company for the past four years in Stockton, where he created and administers the San Joaquin Film Festival as well as the Stockton Speaks crosscultural documentary series. He's also a proficient concert pianist, composer, graphic designer and web programmer.

But unlike most would-be Quentin Tarantinos, Sophoan was born on the dirt floor of a tent in a refugee camp on the border of Cambodia and Thailand in 1985, his family having fled shelling from the Vietnamese Army. Five years later they found sponsorship that brought them to the States, where his father is a minister in the Seventh-Day Adventist church. Sophoan often performs Christian music with family members. "I'm very Americanized, but also very Cambodian," he says. "I'm definitely a Christian, but other than that I appreciate many different cultures and ways of life."

On the phone, Sophoan is so voluble, solicitous and sweet-natured that if I didn't know better I might think he was high. He is outdoors on his cell, running from one activity to another. He first saw Céline on the Oscars in 1997, singing "Because You Loved Me," but he was young at the time "and just listened to what my friends listened to, alternative rock. . . . I didn't know what I wanted." But later, "I heard 'All By Myself' on the radio, and I was blown away by that powerhouse scream—I was like, 'Wow, can a human being do this?' . . . I went online and read her story."

Céline suited his passionate nature: "There's no one else I can find who can sing love songs nonstop." And he admired her for being so family-oriented, "the way she's overcome so much, stuck to her values." He was a quiet person in high school, but by the time he got to college he was bold enough to join web forums to share his opinions: "I'm a caged bird that's been released!" He worried a little bit about "sexual predators" on the forums, but it's been okay. His morality has also been challenged now and then by some of her "skintight outfits" on stage, but he's made his peace. Friends occasionally tease him, "Are you going to marry Céline?" but "because I'm in the right circle, people with good values, good families," it doesn't happen much.

His other tastes include classical music, a lot of contemporary Christian singers, various stars from international *Idol* competitions, LeAnn Rimes, Josh Groban, the British vocal group Lush Life and "the late great Luther Vandross." Maybe this is a standard set of enthusiasms for a young, music-besotted Christian American today, but I feel as if I'm on the phone to a parallel universe. Then Sophoan adds the *pièce de résistance*: "Oh, and I love Phil Collins. During the time I was living in the refugee camp, 'Groovy Kind of Love' I remember so fondly in my head, even though I couldn't speak a word of English and I was only five." I don't hate Phil Collins, but what on earth does his goopiest tune, "Groovy Kind of Love," sound like to a displaced

Cambodian five-year-old? (I suppose not knowing the word "groovy" would help.)

When I ask what he'd like to see her do in the future, aside from acting in a Sophoan Sorn-directed movie, he says, "She could travel the world and be an ambassador for the UN." Sophoan feels his own work needs not only to represent Cambodian-Americans but in some way eventually to aid Cambodia itself. "And Céline is an epitome of how a person can develop into such a great person but remain grounded. That's how I want to be, and help so many people. But we only have a short life—we've gotta make success fast."

As we say our goodbyes after an hour, we agree that next time we're in the city, we should meet for coffee. I mean it, too. Sophoan is one of the nicest people I've ever talked to. And yet it is one of the most surreal "taste shock" experiences I've had: I couldn't fathom where to begin challenging his perceptions or comparing them to mine. Nor would I want to. His taste world is coherent and an enormous pleasure to him. Not only does it seem as valid as my own, utterly incompatible tastes, I like him so much that for a long moment his taste seems *superior*. What was the point again of all that nasty, life-negating crap I like?

* * *

Seeking slightly more familiar territory, my next interview is with a Vegas drag queen. One of the fascinating aspects of Céline is that despite her origins in a rural conservative Catholicism, and not doing anything in particular to encourage the identification, she has become a gay icon. I was curious how a gay man who dresses up and imitates Céline on stage night after night would describe the appeal.

Alex Serpa performs in Las Vegas's longest-running drag cabaret, the "What a Drag" revue at the Freezone club. He was born in Havana, where his mother worked as an extra in TV shows, "so I was always around performers and backstage." He started out as a Barbra impersonator, then expanded to Cher. In about 1996, a friend told him he looked kind of like Céline Dion. "Who?" said Alex. But he started digging around. Now Céline is Alex's favorite character to perform, partly because he makes more in tips. "With Céline the audience has more of a tendency to get up and groove with the music. With Cher, they would just sit there and, 'Oh yes, Cher.' With Céline they get up and go, 'Okay! Woo!' People get up and start to clap, and that's very rare for people to do with drag shows."

A lot of the key is in the pose: "You can tell from a silhouette that it's Céline Dion. She stands with her hip off, and the Elvis leg out. That's where you start, how you let them know it's Céline Dion. . . . My word for her is 'kooky,' in a good way."

As for the gay following, "It's probably more of an older gay crowd than the younger kids . . . being she's so mellow most of the time—her music is fireplace-and-champagne music." But it is decidedly camp. "I wouldn't say a theatrical camp. More of a comedical, caricature camp."

Alex is a female impersonator, not a queer-studies professor. When I ask him what he thinks about haters jibing that Céline herself looks like a drag queen, he says he doesn't see it. But then he adds: "I do think she's impersonating other celebrities . . . Elvis. Tina Turner. Barbra Streisand. Her hand mannerisms are Barbra. The energy is all very Tina. These were the people she grew up wanting to be, taking the best from each person and incorporating it into your act."

After all, he says, "There's no such thing as originality. It's all been done."

* * *

My last interview is a whole other bag. Stephanie Verge and I didn't meet online, but through friends at an experimental-theater performance. She's an attractive woman in her late twenties, an arts-listings editor at a prominent Toronto magazine. When our friend mentions my book and it comes out that Stephanie is a Céline fan, she's well aware how improbable it seems. When we meet later, she explains she grew up in a mixed French-English family in a small francophone town outside of Ottawa. When it comes to her and her younger sister's Céline fandom, each branch of the family disavows it—"the English ones say it must be a French thing, and the French ones say it must be the English side of me warping my mind." At her grandfather's funeral, in the Quebec village where her dad grew up, she got into a conversation about Céline with the driver all the way to the funeral home, as her father shrank into his seat. "It was clear [the driver and I] loved her in different ways, though. He was talking about how close she is to her family, how he saw her grow up in the media, still makes French albums, and so on."

Stephanie's responses are a lot more layered. She recalls grade one at her French Catholic school, when she got obsessed with the song Céline sang for the Pope, *Un colombe*, the first popular song she ever listened to, outside of the Beatles and Broadway-soundtrack albums her parents (a teacher and a civil servant) had at home. "It was my first taste of, 'Oh, this is what other people are listening to. There's some kind of cultural currency here and now I'm a part of it.'" As a teenager, she got into folk music (Laura Nyro, Emmylou Harris) and only came around to Céline again when she had moved to Toronto for university and started dating a woman who "had the tastes of a really, really, really gay man." It was an obsession they could share, but also for Stephanie a lifeline to her French background in an English environment.

Though she has an ironic distance about it, it's not the kind of irony that makes cool dudes wear hair-metal T-shirts. Stephanie loves Céline, and from a dozen angles: "She really does high drama like few others . . . like the lunge, I enjoy the lunge, and the fistpumping is good." But in the next breath: "I respect the fact that she hasn't changed that much over the years. She's still really, really, really small-town, lower-class, and I mean this in the best way, *Québécoise*." And again: "The fact that she's still inappropriate, like that whole Larry King thing, have you watched that? It kills me, it does. It's like watching a car crash but it comes from such a good place."

Stephanie isn't an intense music fan in general, and her Céline fixation "goes in waves. It really does depend on who I'm hanging out with. . . . But I like it in a way that I don't think she's an idiot. I mean, I watch it to laugh at her, because I think she's funny and ridiculous. But I still sort of respond to her emotionally." The French music is more moving to her and the English music more camp, though "the French stuff is pretty camp, too. . . . I think it's just that some really weird, twisted part of me thinks that this is my cultural heritage. Which it's not, because no one in my family is like that."

She doesn't, in fact, have kitschy tastes in general. She admits a weakness for teen movies, but she spends more time reading serious literature. She goes to experimental theater. Still, "the concept of trying to know who the next-big-thing is just seems so difficult and exhausting. . . . And if someone goes, 'You don't like that, you're not cool,' I'm like, 'I'm not cool. That's okay.' . . . I'm fine with my obsessions because I don't think it makes me any less intelligent."

The one time she felt a twinge of shame, she says, is when she was dating someone recently "who has I guess what would be considered really quite good taste in music. She's discerning. . . . And there was one of those moments where I was like, 'Oh man. She thinks I am so lame.' . . . I think I saved myself with a reference to [Boston singer-songwriter] Martin Sexton or something—which is neither here nor there on the cool scale, but certainly cooler than Céline."

She even admits that there's a streak of snobbery in her antisnobbery. "I just don't like being told what I want. It almost comes full circle: People who go out of their way to make sure they don't listen to anything mainstream, they've been told, 'You're supposed to like this,' and then they're like, 'I don't want to like this.' But then these people have their *own* 'Céline,' and everyone is supposed to like that.. . . . I say, 'It's basically your version of Céline. I don't like it. I like *Céline!*' I do admit to having a bit of a hate-on for people who have hipster hobbies, hipster tastes. It makes me want to go in the other direction—although I don't always. There are obviously things that intersect."

I ask her if she feels any identification with Céline fans in general. "I guess part of me feels a solidarity with other people who like her, even though we would never probably have anything to talk about outside of that. But that they just don't care that other people are laughing at them. . . ."

She pauses, and says, "I tend to feel oddly defensive about people who put down big movements, unless they're horribly offensive big movements." It's wrapped up, she says, with how she feels about the Catholic Church. Stephanie isn't a practicing Catholic, and is very critical of the church, but her family is made up of "well-educated," "reflective" people who still have immense faith. She resents friends who "assume it means they're idiots."

"I think we live in a society where people's visceral responses or emotional responses aren't really respected. And I think they should be," she says. "Even if it's not cool, even if it borders on the ridiculous in a lot of ways, and you can't imagine why people would ever cry to a Céline Dion song, I think we should probably have more of a respect for people's lack of guile. . . . I think it's good to have things that you can't explain."

* * *

In the preshow of Céline's multimedia extravaganza at Caesar's Palace in Las Vegas, the stage appears to be over-hung by a mammoth gilded picture frame, within which is a real-time, live-video projection of us, the audience. As show time nears, the camera zooms in on selected spectators, creating a serial comic pantomime in which we get to catch people catch themselves being caught on camera and flinch in embarrassment or mug for our amusement. First it's three girls in J'ADORE DION T-shirts; then two low-key parents with their daughter (Dad is reading a book and never even notices his fifteen seconds); then an impressively tanked pair, the guy's shirt half-unbuttoned and the woman with huge silicon boobs; last, a couple still wearing their wedding outfits. And at that, the frame, which is merely a computer-generated illusion on North America's largest indoor LED screen, expands and shatters into a thousand shards of glassy light, which all spin tinkling through the air and converge . . . on Céline herself, revealed poised atop a sweeping red staircase.

I hardly needed to see the rest of the show. It was a perfect figure of music calling forth, representing, breaking and remaking identities. Céline was offering to reflect us back to ourselves, with all our endearing foibles but larger, fancier, better. She put an eighteenth-century golden frame around us, the ultimate in egalitarian bling, then shattered our collective self to draw the fragments into her own body, itself little but a container for her voice, its own kind of exquisite antique. Yet the frame was long out of fashion—no elite connoisseur or curator would fix it to a contemporary picture. And this, I thought, in my cut-price balcony seat, is why Céline winds up mocked, because her efforts at class and taste always go wrong. With her synthesized strings and genuine pearls and her opera-crossover attempts, she aspires to the highbrow culture of a half-century ago. She doesn't pass the retina scan: the real elites now are busy affecting muttonchops and trucker caps and reading about teen pop in *The New Yorker.*

But the fact is, *A New Day,* which I'd been dreading as I boarded the plane, was the most fun I had the whole trip. Céline was gawky and funny and, compared to most of Vegas, human-scale. I liked it best when she came downstage, out of the knot of dancers and numbingly literal CGI projections that illustrated every song, to chat a bit stiffly and accept flowers. It was easy then to see that she was Canadian, and we could be un-American and uncool together, along with the tiny Filipino mom who sat beside me whispering, "Wow. Oh wow," and occasionally weeping behind the sunglasses that she wore, sitting in the dark, the whole show. Her oversized shades reminded me of Phil Spector and the lost Céline recordings, and I started to get sucked in by the music, too. The songs of devotion—"If You Asked Me To" or "Because You Loved Me"—began to probe at the open sore of my own recent marital separation, and even coaxed a few tears. For a few moments, I got it. Of course, then Céline would do something unforgiveable, like a duet with an enormous projection of the head of the late Frank Sinatra. Still, I could see the *point* of her in Vegas, land of ejaculating slot machines and flows of global capital through artificial rivers: *Let them touch these things!*

And I could answer, *Yes, touch me, Céline.*

But when I had escaped from Vegastraz, back home in Toronto with her CDs, I couldn't find the feeling again.

10.
Let's Do a Punk Version of "My Heart Will Go On" (or, Let's Talk About Our Feelings)

There's a portentous overture of bass, and then those flesh-eatingly familiar notes—*dah-dah-deee, yi-ee-da-doe-daah* . . . except that this time they are not tootling from a penny whistle but snapped out on electric guitar, like Jimi Hendrix unfurling his "Star-Spangled Banner." Then the guitarist stutters into power chords and the singer staggers into the lyrics in a nosy, melodic mewl: "Everrrrynightin*my*dreams! I *see*you! I *feel*you! ThatishowIknow you go-woah *awnnn!*" Chug-chug, chug-chug, *kick*-drum, *kick*-drum.

Along with this one by Florida-bred mall punks New Found Glory, I know of at least five more punkish covers of "My Heart Will Go On" in circulation, by Australia's Screaming Jets, Nashville group Los Straitjackets (a twangy instrumental), Orange County's the Vandals, Los Angeles's snotty, "girlcentric" Switchblade Kittens and New Jersey spoof-metal band Satanicide (the closest to the original, since it just puts Céline's metal-on-estrogen back on testosterone). I bet many more have been done live by bands that never went so far as to record them. The rite of the punk or "ironic" cover goes back at least (not counting Hendrix) to the Sex Pistols covering the Monkees' "Stepping Stone," a middle-finger thrust at commercial disposability that's given a twist by the realization that the Pistols themselves were, like the Monkees, a "manufactured" band. The ironic cover might have come into full bloom when post-punk group the Replacements took to playing tunes by Kiss and other arena-rock bands in their early-80s club shows, as my friend Jake London claimed in a 1996 lost classic of rock criticism called "Sucking in the Seventies: Paul Westerberg, The Replacements and the Onset of the Ironic Cover Aesthetic in Rock'n'Roll." Jake, a Seattle musician and lawyer, thinks ironic covers allowed post-baby-boom "underground" rock scenes to smuggle the repudiated music of their childhoods back into their lives: at first you'd ask if the Replacements were kidding or if they "really" liked Kiss, but with repetition, the jokey protective bubble would wear away, until Kiss seemed just plain *good* again, like they did when you were ten. It undermined the canons laid down by boomer rock criticism, and in time a lot of other outcast music was reclaimed this way: a band with the Midas touch of cool, like Sonic Youth, could overturn scenester vilification of Madonna just by releasing an EP of covers as Ciccone Youth.

Today the ironic cover's dominant form is the acoustic or rearranged version of a current hit—say, Kelly Clarkson's "Since U Been Gone." It still gets club crowds chuckling nervously, but there's a more charitable tone: at worst it says, "There's a good tune under all that cheese"; often it's just, "Fuck that, I love this song." Likewise, the punk cover's more high-tech successor, the mashup, often showcases the "good parts" of a hit, digitally spliced into a cooler song: when

Christina Aguilera's "Genie in a Bottle" was mashed with the Strokes' "Can't Explain," it won her a lot of converts. Meta-criticism in musical form, both covers and mashups help siphon the guilt out of guilty pleasures. But not for Céline. Punk covers of her acidly musicalize the vitriol she gets in the press. The only Céline mashup I've heard blends "My Heart Will Go On" with moody Icelandic band Sigur Ros, and the subtext isn't "look, Céline's okay," but "look, you stupid Sigur Ros fans, they're as boring as Céline Dion." Cover-version irony fails as a gateway to redemption because her music, much more than "dumb" rock, teen-pop or the cartoon-thug side of hip-hop, is exactly what hip defenses exist to guard against: it's sentimental.

For a century or more, sentimentality has been the cardinal aesthetic sin. To say a work of art is sentimental is perforce to damn it. To be sentimental is to be kitsch, phony, exaggerated, manipulative, self-indulgent, hypocritical, cheap and clichéd. It is the art of religious dupes, conservative apologists and corporate stooges. As kitsch, it is likened to fascist or Stalinist propaganda by Milan Kundera, Clement Greenberg, Harold Rosenberg, Dwight Macdonald and of course Theodor Adorno. The German novelist Hermann Broch wrote, "The producer of kitsch does not produce 'bad' art. . . . It is not quite impossible to assess him according to aesthetic criteria; rather he should be judged as an ethically base being, a malefactor who profoundly desires evil." The punk sneer pronounces the same verdict. And all things considered, perhaps because I'm a lyrics listener, sentimentality is also the most formidable barrier between Céline's music and me: it's not just that the Hallmark-card messages are unappealing, but a fear that yielding to them may turn my brain and principles to mush. Can that really be just learned prejudice, like so many other cultural filters?

To be sure, I can absolve sentimentality of the superficial charges fast. Manipulative? Manipulating listeners, *moving* them, is what music is supposed to do, skillfully. Phony? All art is fake. What matters is to be a convincing fake, a lie that feels true. Clearly Céline has her audience convinced. And is her soundtrack-to-your-life approach more "self-indulgent" than James Joyce's multilingual word games? Is that really a fault in art? Who else should the artist be indulging? As for hypocrisy: certainly, dressing Nazism up with rosy-cheeked mothers and children frolicking on German hillsides is disgusting, but what's wrong with rosy-cheeked mothers and kids if they're not Nazis? Taking mere mawkishness as propaganda is paranoid, absent a specific evil it's complicit in, unless you extend that indictment to any art not made explicitly as protest. (For a more rigorous rundown of these arguments, see the late American moral philosopher Robert C. Solomon's *In Defense of Sentimentality*.)

A more thoughtful question is one of proportion: is the problem that kitsch sentimentality (in musical terms, schmaltz) takes everyday hopes and affections and inflates them into life-or-death melodramas? Consider Zen scholar R. H. Blyth's elegant definition, "We are being sentimental when we give to a thing more tenderness than God gives to it." This is the antisentimentality John Cage enacted by composing music based on random rolls of dice, to subtract his own will from the outcome—his silent piece, *3'33"*, is just a frame to focus the ears and mind on the sounds of existence already in progress. His music is beautiful in its willingness to surrender itself to that objectivity. Like Cage's silence,

God's love is unspeakable, implacable, its gaze matter-of-fact. But human love is something else: We love in excess of God's love if we love at all. We love by heaping meaning on objective fact. If I believed in God, I might imagine this is what He created humans for, to give things more tenderness than He granted them, amid nature's unblinking harshness and the cruelty of fate—perhaps we are here to make up for what Depeche Mode, in its Gnostic pop song "Blasphemous Rumors," called God's "sick sense of humor." God's love might sound like Kraftwerk, a sonic diagram of passing traffic, or the relentless electronic march of a disco track by Giorgio Moroder, but humanity is the Donna Summer vocal that cannot resist muscling in to overstate the obvious, to exalt the obvious in hallucinatory helixes, insisting over and over, "I feel love, I feel love, I feel love." God or no God, it's hubris to pretend to know the correct amount of tenderness it is ours to grant.

Aesthetically, too, excess seems an old-fashioned concern, unless excess tenderness is more reprehensible than the excesses of paint, noise, rage, monumentality, vocabulary, nakedness and more that art has rolled around in since modernism and especially since rock'n'roll, much to our delight. When a critic says Céline "bulldozes" a song, it's a plaint; when a critic says, "The Ramones bulldoze through a three-minute punk pounder," that's praise. Cliché certainly might be an aesthetic flaw, but it's not what sets sentimentality apart in pop music, or there wouldn't be a primitive band every two years that's hailed for bringing rock "back to basics."

Such double standards arise everywhere for sentimental music: excess, formulaism, two-dimensionality can all be positives for music that is not gentle and conciliatory, but infuriated and rebellious. You could say punk rock is anger's schmaltz—a notion reinforced by how easily, with "emo" punk, it is refitted to express personal angst. Punk, metal, even social-justice rock such as U2 or Rage Against the Machine, with their emphatic slogans of individuality and independence, are as much "inspirational" or "motivational" music as Céline's is, but for different subcultural groups. They are just as one-sided and unsubtle. Morally you could fairly ask what is more laudable about excess in the name of rage and resentment than immoderation in thrall to love and connection. The likely answer would be that Céline is conformist, quiescent, unsubversive. "Subversion" today is sentimentality's inverse: It is nearly always a term of approval. To show the subversiveness of a song, TV show or movie is tantamount to validating it, not just in pop criticism but in academic scholarship.

What is subversive? Transgression, satire, idiosyncracy, radicalism, asserting a minority identity, throwing noise into the signal, upending convention, generally mitigating for *change.* But as social critic Thomas Frank (*The Conquest of Cool*) has long argued, today those are values promoted by advertising, corporate-management gurus and high-tech entrepreneurs. Canadian authors Joseph Heath and Andrew Potter's entertaining polemic *The Rebel Sell* adds that anticonformist impulses are the octane of consumerism, seeking the cutting edge, the very soul of Bourdieuvian distinction, whether in designer couture, organic cuisine or "uncommodified" culture. Thus there is now, and maybe always was, a conservative vibration in the heartbeat of rock'n'rebellion. Corporate and government rhetoric mimics and migrates into rebel schmaltz. The kind of change implored in the music of strident sarcasm—freedom, equality, less authority—aligns handily with a "new economy" whose trade and labor-market needs require a more "flexible," mobile, multicultural social structure. Capitalism today cheers decentralization, deregulation and other conspicuous change that spikes short-term stock prices and justifies layoffs, unpaid overtime, third-world outsourcing and ubiquitous marketing, plus the organized violence that supports them. Naomi Klein's book *The Shock Doctrine* points to a continuum between economic, political, military and torture-room "shock therapy"—might the metaphor extend to the artistic "shock of the new"?

Music criticism's attachment to youth rebellion is not free of these myopias: what liberal critics label subversive seldom pertains to practical social reform. In fact, the few critics with larger political commitments often attend more sympathetically to mass culture, even the supposedly bland and sentimental sort, because their concerns involve human lives, not cultural one-upmanship. Which is not a bad yardstick to sort politics from revolutionary playacting.

Even in the ostensibly more serious realm of academia, notably Cultural Studies, the idea of "resistant" reading—that audiences make self-empowering, anti-establishment reinterpretations of mainstream culture—can be merely a reverse justification of personal taste. An academic who likes Kelly Clarkson will find cause to claim she offers more recoupably resistant material than Britney Spears. It may be that, as Bourdieu believed, aesthetics are mostly a disguise for political relationships. But to then use politics as a further disguise for your aesthetics is to build a hall of mirrors. Since power is a dynamic that permeates even the most microscopic interactions, you can find submission or resistance in any cultural figure or artifact if you look; but it can be misleading to do so selectively, and break pop culture down into quiescent versus subversive blocs.

Why, finally, should subversion be the *sine qua non*? Fans, after all, are not always busy resisting and recontextualizing their idols—they also support, defend and identify with them. If we disavow a Kantian formal aesthetic, a "disinterested" gaze, then whenever someone says an artwork is good or bad, it is reasonable to ask "good or bad for what?" What's the *usefulness* of Céline's music for her fans, if it is not about subversion? Lawrence W. Levine has written that appraising art by its novelty or radicalism is "a modern fallacy contradicted by the centuries of folk artists who saw their function as embodying the beliefs and meanings of their cultures in language that could be understood by their fellows." Sentimentality in popular art is one of the few vectors along which this "folk" function still can be fulfilled: "Art can just as legitimately stand near the center of common experience and give its audiences a sense of recognition and community."

In that light, mightn't Céline's music of everyday affirmation also have social value? Her songs are often about the struggle of sustaining an emotional reality, about fidelity, faith, bonding and survival—continuity, that is, in the destabilizing flux of late capitalism. While business and rebel-schmaltz stars alike tout self-realization, social negation and the delegitimation of traditional values, Céline's music (like Nashville country) tends to prioritize "recognition and community," connection and solidarity. Granted, she also promotes overwork, ambition and luxury, which is to say she's still a pop star. But in that matrix, sentimentality might be her greatest virtue.

That's a painful admission, because it implies that the

shelter for oddness and dissatisfaction that maverick art and culture have offered in my life may be self-servingly segregating and undemocratic. It pours cold water on the hope that art that insists on its quirky independence fosters critical thinking, even models social change. Art's shock tactics do clear ground for cultural shifts, but what artists foresee is seldom what society gets. Certainly, celebrities like Céline can help advertise an American Dream cover story for a destructive hegemony by appealing to widely held desires and aspirations. But the transgressive individualism of modernism's heirs verges on directly emulating that destructive drive, while *jeering* at its victims' aspirations and desires. Maybe I have met the Ugly American, and he is me.

The most compelling indictment of sentimentality in art is that it distorts reality by expunging the darker side. In a famous passage in his novel *The Unbearable Lightness of Being*, Milan Kundera writes that kitsch is "the absolute denial of shit, in both the literal and the figurative senses of the word; kitsch excludes everything from its purview which is essentially unacceptable in human existence." But in much of modern, critically certified art, what happens is a denial of *non*shit, of everything that is *acceptable* in human existence. On a political level, one might ask if this equal and opposite distortion doesn't breed hopelessness and passivity. As Robert C. Solomon says, "Why should we *always* be made aware of flaws and dangers? . . . Should we make it a point never to have a nice thought without a nasty one as well?"

The very greatest art may ball all the shit and nonshit of existence together, the way it comes in life, but on the less exalted tiers, why must art that focuses mainly on what Solomon calls "the tender emotions" take a back seat to art that focuses mainly on the harsh ones? The hierarchies of anti-sentimentalism seem to end in a perverse reversal of values. As Canadian philosopher Deborah Knight suggests in her 1999 paper, "Why We Enjoy Condemning Sentimentality," one cause is macho rationalism. If the tender emotions are stereotypically feminine, cuddly, nurturing, then the sentimental, as she puts it, is "sluttish"—"indulgent, cheap, shallow, self-absorbed, excessive." Philosophical antisentimentalism, she asserts, is a sentimentalization of rationalism, a pre-emptive strike against betraying any unseemly weakness for the illogical, girly side of human nature. (And it doesn't get much more girly than Céline Dion.)

And even if the gender bias is receding, it's not the only social ranking involved: mastering one's emotions is also a time-honored upper-class imperative. There's a reason cool is called "cool," and within its economy, it's not just, to swipe the title of a 1980s famine-relief anthem, that "Tears Are Not Enough," but that tears are almost always too much. If you put down "cheap thrills" today, you're a stuffy old snob, but you're far more free to vent distinctionalist contempt for sentiment's "cheap emotion."

It's often assumed that audiences for schmaltz are somehow stunted, using sentimental art as a kind of emotional crutch. As Solomon points out, there's no evidence for this slur: isn't it equally plausible that people uncomfortable with representations of vulnerability and tenderness have emotional problems? Sentimental art can be a rehearsal, a workout to keep emotions toned and ready for use. This doesn't dictate that those uses will be appropriate ones, and emotions alone are not solutions to issues, but sympathy and compassion are prerequisites to charity and solidarity. So

CARL WILSON

between the sentimentalist and the antisentimentalist, who is the real emotional cripple?

Me, for one. The underlying reason I had such a bad time in Vegas was not that it was tacky: it was that the tackiness made me feel even lonelier than I already was, some six months after my marriage dissolved. For a moment in the Colosseum, beside the teary Filipino mom, Céline helped me feel that big, dumb emotion on a gut level. My usual, more "sophisticated" listening can help me reflect on such feelings, to scrutinize them from all angles, but I'm fine at that kind of analysis on my own. I am probably less skilled at just feeling an emotion without wanting to mess with it and craft it, to bargain with it until it becomes something else. Feeling emotions fully, bodily, as they are, may be sentimentality's promise, one too readily mistaken for a threat.

I'm not alone in that. At the same Pop Conference panel in which he made his faux pas about "black music, like Céline Dion," songwriter Stephin Merritt argued that "catharsis in art is always embarrassing." It's a common belief, though seldom so drolly expressed. He was partly drawing on Bertolt Brecht, who held that the purgative release of catharsis can defuse social criticism. But like many of us, Merritt transposed that political caveat to a personal one, a matter of style. His enjoyment, he claimed only half-joshingly, depends on having the embarrassment built into the art, as irony, which allows him to register emotion without the shameful loss of self-control involved in *feeling* it. Here we reach a crossroads where sophistication is just another word for paralyzing repression. It's as if we've mangled one nostrum of craft, which warns against artists "expressing themselves" by just blurting emotions out confessionally, into another (an)aesthetic principle that art should not be expressive or cathartic *for the audience.*

Kundera similarly rails against sentimentality for subjecting the sovereign individual to the humiliation of feeling human: "Kitsch causes two tears to flow in quick succession. The first tear says: *How nice to see children running on the grass!* The second tear says: *How nice to be moved, together with all mankind, by children running on the grass!* It is the second tear that makes kitsch kitsch." What he dismisses as self-congratulation here, as Solomon notes, is the way sentimental catharsis (like the tragic kind) might prompt contemplation of universal experience, arguably the starting place of philosophy. And Kundera's own self-congratulation practically reeks from the page.

What self-conscious aesthetes such as Kundera, Merritt and I might be guilty of sentimentalizing is ambiguity, that shibboleth of our postidealistic age. Which can make us dupes of another kind, prone to taking surface complication and opacity for depth, and apt to overlook the complexity that may lie even within the sentimental on more patient, curious inspection. It's a fault endemic, I think, to us antireligionists who have turned for transcendent experience to art, and so react to what our reflexes tell us is bad art as if it were a kind of blasphemy.

It's not that sentimental art can't be lousy. Nothing can convince me that the book Céline produced with photographer Anne Geddes, *Miracle*—full of color-saturated pictures of newborns lying limp in Céline's arms and in the pods of overgrown vegetables—is anything but grotesque, an unusual lapse into the total narcissism of which critics accuse her, which I can excuse only as the temporary insanity of new parenthood. (She and René had a lot of trouble conceiving, finally resorting to invitro fertilization.) But what makes the book bad is not that it says babies are special. Babies *are* special: They represent continuity. They call for our protection. They present a mysterious otherness to the fallenness and compromise of socialized life. They're adorable. And Kundera be damned, it can enlarge our tolerance and fellow feeling to be reminded that other people, even real assholes, are mostly with us on the baby issue. What is wrong here is that the book makes the infants look like little dead space aliens laid out for autopsy in a prefabishly fecund Organic Garden of Eden.

It is what's done with sentiment, like any other inspiration, that can be an aesthetic liability, not sentiment itself. To muddle the two is to risk coarsening ourselves against, in Lincoln's phrase, the better angels of our nature. What's more, as Saul Bellow wrote, "Everybody knows there is no fineness or accuracy of suppression; if you hold down one thing, you hold down the adjoining." So what else, in pushing down the sentimental, might we lose access to? Anne Geddes's pictures will not deter us from cooing over real babies. But what of the fact that it is hard to imagine a male performer today having a hit by singing about his mother, at one time a regular occurrence in popular song? Is that topic inherently less artful than singing about fucking? No, but outside of country music, that last refuge of parlor-song verities, the spectre of sentimentality scares us off, and motherhood's exile from our music becomes one more way we take our moms for granted.

Canadian filmmaker Guy Maddin once said, "I think that melodrama isn't just life exaggerated, but life uninhibited." It's a provocative thought: that the melodramatic, the sentimental, might be a repressed truth of human feeling, inhibited by the modern imperatives of reason and ambiguity. Perhaps the dream content of the sentimental is today in need of liberation, the way that in the early twentieth century, Freud and the surrealists realized western society needed to bare and scratch the sexual, violent underbelly of consciousness. With inhibitions against them removed, the tender sentiments might unveil their unsuspected splendors.

For that, though, we would have to relax our constant vigil against looking or feeling ridiculous. Céline herself addresses that hurdle on the first single from her 2007 album *D'Elles*, "*Et s'il n'en restait qu'une*," with lyrics by French novelist Françoise Doiron. She sings that "if there remained only one person" who was willing to "stupidly" trace hearts in the sand, wish on stars, "envy the carousels where boys and girls have fallen in love since the beginning of time" and dream under the moonlight, she "would be that one." This song, which laughs at the clichédness of cliché but then defiantly embraces it, is Céline's rebuttal to the sneers of critics and punk singers—to, as Solomon puts it, "the enormous amount of sophistry that is devoted to making fun of and undermining the legitimacy of such emotions."

That barrage of ridicule can seem daunting, but remember that, in other instances, so frivolous a gesture as an ironic punk-rock cover has managed to melt scorn gradually into fond attachment. In his 2002 essay "On Being Laughed At," British psychoanalyst Adam Phillips writes: "We only laugh at those with whom we feel we have an affinity that we must repudiate. . . . We laugh to sabotage our feeling of being at one with; but the feeling of at-oneness has already happened. It is a question, as it often is, of imagined catastrophe; what, we must ask, is the imagined devastation that will occur if the mocker doesn't mock? If he isn't laughing at his victim, if he stops arranging his humiliation, what does he fear might happen? What might they do together? The so-called psychological answer might be, he will see too much of himself, too much of something about himself, in his chosen victim. The political answer would be, he would turn democratic. What mockery reveals, in other words, is the emotional terror of democracy. That what is always being ridiculed is our wish to be together, our secret affinity for each other."

One afternoon early in our relationship, my future ex-wife and I were lazing around her small apartment, listening to music. Testing boundaries, I began teasing her a bit about her music collection, mostly thrift-shop copies of 50s crooner and rock'n'roll records, a quaint-seeming fixation for a twenty-four-year-old downtown novelist. She went over to the suitcase record player and put "Oh Boy" by Buddy Holly under the worn-out needle: "All of my life I've been a-waitin' / Tonight there'll be no hesitatin'—oh boy! When you're with me . . ." And she sang along: "Stars appear and shadows are falling / You can hear my heart a-calling / A little bit of lovin' makes everything right / I'm gonna see my baby tonight!" She loved it, she said, because it was the truth. There was nothing more layered or contradictory to say. "Oh boy!" expressed exactly how she felt, right there and then, about me.

I don't think I have ever been more moved, even in our wedding vows, by a profession of love. I've seldom felt so honored, so human, so sure that merely human was enough. That it did not remain enough, that there would be a sadder side to the story, does nothing to mar it, nor to diminish one watt in my memory the soft autumn light that fell across her face as she sang Buddy Holly's words to me.

All right, Céline, I'm ready. Bring it on.

11.
Let's Talk About
Let's Talk About Love

You don't know what an egotistical control freak your taste can be until you try to turn traitor, as witness the slapstick contortions I've had to resort to just to get myself to listen to Céline Dion. Right now her 2003 Roy Orbison cover, "I Drove All Night," is pouring out of my speakers, and I can barely resist flicking out my hand to switch it off. It's not that it offends me personally anymore—I even have some crackpot theories about how Roy was like Céline, male drag king to her female drag queen. No, the problem is that my building is so poorly soundproofed. It's a converted industrial space (cliché, I know) and to move in, I had to sign a waiver accepting noise levels higher than allowed by municipal codes. Whenever my neighbors argue, watch TV, have sex or listen to techno, I hear it. And I know that they hear me. It's a minor voyage of self-discovery: for instance, it turns out that I am not so bothered by having strangers hear me have sex, compared to how embarrassed I am by having them hear me play *Let's Talk About Love* over and over. I worry that it annoys them, but mainly that they're thinking, "What a loser." It took months before I could bring myself to play it openly at full volume, rather than through headphones or some other subterfuge. Unwittingly, I seem to have converted Céline from a guilty displeasure into a classic guilty pleasure, a category I thought I'd thrown away long ago.

Yes, I said pleasure. In ways. At times. By way of explanation, let's pose a more cumulative question: How, taking all our investigations so far into account, would I write a review of *Let's Talk About Love*? Could I manage not to take the transparency of taste as a given, or to stake out a superior, disinterested position? What sort of aesthetic calls could I still make? Since it would be artificial to pretend the record is new, let's imagine as a pretext that *LTAL* is being reissued for its tenth anniversary in the year of this writing, 2007, and that a magazine has assigned me a feature about it. Here it is, the penultimate stage of our experiment.

* * *

Céline Dion
Let's Talk About Love: Aluminum Anniversary Edition
(Sony Music)
Reviewed by Carl Wilson for *33 1/3* magazine

If pop music were a Tarot deck, Céline Dion would be the Three of Swords—triple blades thrust through a bulging red heart, the sky raining down tears. Her role in the daytrading, dot-comming late 1990s (when *Let's Talk About Love* became her second straight album to sell 20-million-plus) was to balance the era's "irrational exuberance" by giving the limbic system a colonic: a hearty, cleansing cry. But I never took her cure.

It's not that I'm some immovable stoic. If you want to know what makes me cry, more reliably than anything this side of George Jones singing "He Stopped Loving Her Today," it's usually some squishy moment from a TV show about a teenage girl. *My So-Called Life, Buffy the Vampire Slayer, Veronica Mars, Freaks and Geeks, Joan of Arcadia* . . . You name them, they've turned my waterworks on.

I have an idea why. It isn't just the sad pretty girls. Nor is it, as I first thought, just an escapist return to the febrile ordeals of adolescence, the scene of the crime of self-invention (but through female eyes, because the teen male is not exactly renowned for his psychological acumen). No, the truth is that my so-called adult life is mortifyingly similar to that of a teenage girl, or at least the bemused existentialists who stand in for them on TV: It's a comedy-drama, centered more on groups of friends than family or workplace. The loose plotlines are mainly an excuse for endless talk about relationships, books, bands, What It All Means and how far we can bend the grownup rules before landing in trouble. Usually we bend them too far. My work entails spending a lot of time at cultural events and parties, figuring out how to assimilate to new social groups, to which the answer is always: Awkwardly. With a lot of crushes. But my life is also guided by a vocation, a secret mission like Buffy's (vampire slayer) or Veronica's (girl detective) or Joan's (special envoy for God). Mine just involves more typing and less stalking the undead. This is where the grislier side of the identification comes in: the mission tends to distance me from the center ring of adult life, the hurlyburly of business and domesticity, where the normal grownups live. All of which, I fear, has arrested my development.

It's an increasingly common affliction. Cultural fields have always broken into style-based cliques (once known precisely as "schools"), so they are bound to feel like reruns of teendom. But with current western middle-class trends of prolonged education, delayed marriage and late childbearing, extended adolescence is becoming the norm. In pop culture, that means among other things that high-school-style identity subgroups have turned into permanent consumer-niche categories. I am not pleased about it, but I admit I'm part of it.

Céline Dion, however, is not, which might explain why she's left me dry-eyed. Hell, Dion never even *went* to high school: she'd already dropped out to pursue show biz, as the best hope of her impoverished, fourteen-sibling, French-Canadian family. The entertainment sector she joined was that holdover from the days before pop went subcultural, "adult contemporary." On *Let's Talk About Love*, at twenty-nine, she was duetting with the Bee Gees, Barbra Streisand and Luciano Pavarotti, people in their fifties, sixties and seventies. She didn't know from youth culture. But that also meant she could appeal to grandmas, moms, uncles and dads as well as teen girls (real live ones, who didn't come with wry voiceovers). In this way Dion was the most representative of late-90s musicians. You can hear a zeitgeist throughout this album, find it reflected in the commemorative metallic sheen Sony has wrapped around this anniversary CD/DVD set.

Dion's signature power ballads, on this album including "The Reason," "When I Need You" and of course the *Titanic* hit "My Heart Will Go On," brim with millennial tension.

Their multiple crescendos are calculated to slingshot the listener up and over some unnamed threat, that waiting historical iceberg, to touch down in the placid waters of the End of History. All you needed, she preached, was love, personally or geopolitically. In the closing benediction here, the title track (composed by a French–British–Canadian coalition), she invokes "people around the world, different faces, different names," linked by "one true emotion that reminds me we're the same." Dion partook of the era's corporatist triumphalism, but her global audience could detect in her tone, that of a non-American whose first language was not English, an awareness that even in the pursuit of prosperity, intimate bonds of family and heritage needed to be preserved, indeed fought for with the ardor of a Joan. If she made it sound like such a feat was as simple as sorting out the misunderstandings in a Meg Ryan romantic comedy, well, it was 1997. Optimism was rife. To hear the children's choir come in on "Let's Talk About Love" is to recall a day when even cynics could not know this was just a calm between the wars, and soon collective identities and market pluralism would be set at each other's throats again.

Her blend of entrepreneurial pluck and domestic yearning also made Dion the chanteuse of the "work-life balance," which more women were struggling with than ever before in the "postfeminist" late 90s, some because they'd made partner at the law firm and others because they were juggling three crappy part-time contracts. The going delusion was that not so great a gap separated these working women, as all would share in the dividends of growth. (Remember "employee participation plans" in which meaningless stock options replaced bonus pay?) No song on *LTAL* answers that aspirational call quite like "Immortality," written by and guest-starring the Bee

Gees, which captures Dion's contradictions so comprehen-
sively as to ascend to the incomprehensible. The refrains purr
of eternity and never saying goodbye, but the verses natter
on about dreams that "must" come true: "I will make them
give it to me," Dion sings, and, "Sorry, I don't have a role for
love to play." Whatever "it" is, she's going for it and leaving a
field strewn with bodies and dear-John postcards. It's kind of
horrific to think people play this song at weddings and funerals. Yet the music—produced by Mariah Carey cohort Walter
Afanasieff with a sultry, hovering, almost samba-like synthetic
pulse (no wonder it hit No. 1 in Brazil)—is all love and no
leaving. And the Gibb brothers' backup vocals are so lambent
that I want to sing along with the gibberish, to go with its
liquid flow into some golden neverland of spiritualized avarice
and transcendental materialism.

All of which makes "Immortality" a more compelling artifact of its time than, say, the deflectionary patter of overedu-
cated/underemployed youth peddled by bands like Pavement.
Although, as part of that cadre, I was and am a Pavement fan,
it's clearer in retrospect what was annoying about them, while
Dion gets less so when you can hear her as a coalescence of
social forces—like Elvis in the 50s. Because it's not diverted
into infinitesimal subcultural maneuvers, this record fixated
on private relationships keeps throwing me back out into the
broader public sphere.

It's a heavily populated one, too. Perhaps because she had
to up the ante after the previous year's *Falling Into You* (which
also motivated the "concept-album" title, as if every English-
language Céline Dion record were not, top to bottom, about
love), this album takes the range-demonstrating diversity of a
typical diva record to loopily eclectic extremes. Like almost

every CD released from the mid-90s to the early 2Ks, it is moronically long, running more than seventy minutes just because it can, but it almost requires that much room to encompass power ballads, soft rock, a Broadway two-hander, R&B, disco, pop-gospel, cod opera, even dancehall reggae. It isn't a concept album: Dion is, like most pop performers including the soul and country and hip-hop greats, much more of a singles artist; indeed nearly half the songs here made the charts in one part of the world or another. Instead, think of it as a variety show, "The Céline Love Revue." If one sketch doesn't suit you, a new routine will come along soon, though the performer will always be Céline Dion. This led critics to denounce her lack of personality, which makes you wonder when we turned against showbiz versatility. Each act also has different producers, and their styles are apt to determine which parts of the show you'll like best.

For me, the Busby Berkeley here is veteran producer Ric Wake, and the two turns I find easiest to love are his dance numbers, unsurprisingly, since I usually prefer dance tunes to windy pop ballads. Still, I was amazed how nimbly the dolorous Three of Swords turns into a sparkly Queen of Disco on "Just a Little Bit of Love," and, astoundingly, a ragamuffin-reggae toaster on "Treat Her Like a Lady." I approached the latter with a textbook's worth of ammunition on cultural appropriation and latterday minstrelsy, but screw it: Sure, Dion may not have known much about the controversy over misogyny in dancehall reggae that occasioned this schoolin'-the-roughnecks tune by Jamaican singer Diana King, but she can get behind the title sentiment. With King on hand interjecting patois and Detroit girl group Brownstone on jump-rope vocals, Dion doesn't seem to be doing a patronizing pastiche; she sounds wiggly, jubilant, her own goofy self. And that there exists a Céline Dion antisexist dancehall-reggae anthem is nothing short of the sort of Ripley's Believe It or Not item that makes it a joy each morning to wake up alive.

The slower song under Wake's direction is also the nearest the album comes to making me cry: "Love is on the Way," an inspirational that actually inspires. The secret is that unlike most positive-thinking seminars in pop form, it anticipates my skepticism and reaches out to shake my shoulders about it: *You're a mess, the world is a mess, what else can you expect, right? Listen up, buddy, you can expect* lots. *Good things are coming to you. You don't deserve it but that's the way it is. That's "the mystery of tomorrow." Love is gonna* seize you up *on wings of fucking* angels. *So be grateful, you bastard.* The gospel styling reinforces the message. Just as churches say God saves even the miserable sinner, the secular lesson is that time doesn't leave anybody out either: no matter how stuck you feel, you still get to go to the future. And when I am morose about my tendency to repeat self-defeating patterns, this music is a reminder that some patterns—a pounding drum fill, a *do-re-mi-fa-mi* hook and climbing choral *ooohs*—are worth repeating, even if you have to wait out the mildly dull verses to get them.

Wake's opposite for me, the villain of *LTAL*, is Dion's most frequent producer, David Foster. Answering complaints about her records being "overproduced," Dion has very smartly said that to her, that's "not a bad thing—it's a big thing, it's big time, it's *Gone with the Wind*." I'm with her when we're talking about the kind of overproduced she gets out of Meatloaf collaborator Jim Steinman, pedal-to-the-heavy-metal numbers like "It's All Coming Back to Me Now" from *Falling Into You*. But Foster's touch seems merely damp, going too far but not taking you anywhere. I don't hate everything he does but I usually find it forgettable in the way that leads critics to call songs "filler." (I also feel that way about the two Corey Hart productions, "Miles to Go" and "Where Is the Love?") To many Dion fans, however, the Foster tracks are the very core of her appeal. Maybe "filler" is just the name we give to songs aimed at the members of the audience who are least similar to us.

For instance, Foster contributes the tepid R&B of "Why Oh Why." I guess it's not his fault that it suffers retroactively from being recorded just when the whole R&B genre was about to mutate into pop's most sonically astounding wonderland. However, I will blame Foster for the two "marquee attraction" tunes. "Tell Him" finds Dion and Barbra Streisand singing the hell out of Foster's wife's lame writing, an ingenue-and-mentor dialogue that is pious and strident where it could have been teasing and saucy. The only kind of intergenerational dialogue it promises is parents having to explain to their offspring that once upon a time, Barbra Streisand was an entertainer. Meanwhile, "I Hate You, Then I Love You" (a Neapolitanized adaptation of Shirley Bassey's sassy-sad 1973 hit "Never Never Never") is inadvertently funny, due to Luciano Pavarotti's starched line readings and Dion's clumsy overacting. I know many folks like these tracks for the vocal performances, but the "prestige" aura puts me off, no doubt because I have trouble understanding why a 1990s pop singer would need to look to Broadway or opera for validation. Then again, Foster might not understand why I think it would be fantastic if Sony Music took Snoop Dogg up on his claim in a recent interview, "I got beats for Céline Dion."

"I Hate You . . ." might even be meant to be tongue-in-cheek, playing dumb, the way Bassey's version partly does before it goes in for the kill. I can't tell. Whenever I go to the sources of Dion's revivals (like the full-body dip in 70s health-food co-op honey that is Leo Sayer's original "When I Need You"), I find them far more charming. I think it's a quaintness gap: the old songs are yellowing snapshots of expired modes of adulthood, but Foster and Dion seem to claim them as viable today, or at least in 1997. Which leaves me flummoxed.

Most of the rest has moments that grab me, then shake me off again, for example "Us," written and produced by Billy Pace. It's a plea to a disenchanted lover to stick around and, as we say in the age of intimacy-as-labor, *work* on the relationship. Dion gives it a bluesy wail: "You say it doesn't matter—then tell me, what does?" and "You say it's never easy—then tell me, what was?" These seem not just fair questions but the very fairest, about the figure/ground ambiguity that makes breakups so dizzying: *All right, I'm lacking, but relative to what? . . . You say you need "space" and "time"? You and whose metaphysics?* But then it continues on for nearly six minutes, from confrontation into harangue into restraining-order territory. Where's that vaudeville hook?

One producer actually outshines Wake, but he only has one song. Because blockbuster records, like 90s dot-com millionaires, prefer squandering their fortunes immediately, it's the first one. "The Reason" was co-composed by old Brill Building hand and 70s *Tapestry* songwriter Carole King, but most consequentially it was produced and arranged by Sir George Martin, Fifth Beatle, shortly before his retirement. The verses are graceful and the chorus unleashes such Jim Steinman–style pyrotechnics that Dion seems to be shouting not just to a lover who's her "reason" to live but to *the reason*, the prime mover, the abstract principle of the expanding universe. But what makes "The Reason" and remakes it over again are what Sir George might call "the middle eights," to which he brings the sort of bogglingly accomplished prestidigitation he pulled off repeatedly on 70s Paul McCartney hits far sillier than this one. ("Live or Let Die," I'm looking at you.)

The first break slips into a minor key and sets up a counter-rhythm in the cello section, ushering the song behind a curtain into the bed chamber: "In the middle of the night," Dion pants (echoed by a hoochy-mama chorus), "I'm going down, 'cause I *adore* you!" That's right, *going down*. Lest you not believe your ears, there's a classic (stunned?) George Martin pause and drum fill before she lets out a stretching, postcoital sigh: "I . . . *want* . . . to *floor* you." And isn't "floor" a fine euphemism there? The second time it all happens again but more so, adding whooping horns and spiraling into a shit-hot guitar solo by Robbie Macintosh of the Pretenders, and the cumulative effect is to invert the self-abasement that might irk you in the lyrics, ensuring that by what must be called the climax, the lady is firmly on top. A tune that starts with a girl kneeling supplicant before a man ends up as a rhapsody to womanly erotic power as the flux at the heart of the cosmos, and as long as you stop yourself from picturing Dion's real-life husband at any point, you have to admit she nails it in more senses than one. Finally, adult entertainment.

Which lands us, finally, in the lair of the beast: "My Heart Will Go On (Love Theme from *Titanic*)." A decade later, while granting James Horner's melody its fetching lilt, it is still hard to hear this song except as a re-enactment of itself, an eternal recursion that, as a million "and on and on" jokes testify, swamps it from title down. Through the billowing familiarity, I find the song near-impossible to see, much less cry about. Except, that is, once . . . when it turned up on a TV series about a teenaged girl.

It was in the last season of *Gilmore Girls*, a show about a bookish teen named Rory and her mother Lorelai. Lorelai was around Rory's age when she got pregnant, left high school and ran off to a small town to raise her daughter alone. Their closeness in years gives them a rare rapport (including shared cool, offbeat tastes in music). One of the themes is that while Rory is unusually mature, parenthood forced her mom to grow up too fast: the real teen-girl protagonist is the mixed-up one still stirring under Lorelai's competent exterior. Earlier in the season, after yet another failed relationship, she impulsively reunited with and married her high-school boyfriend, Rory's father, Chris. But the marriage becomes strained. Chris is jealous, distant, because he isn't convinced Lorelai wants to be there. Her best friend asks her if she's positive Chris is wrong, and Lorelai can't answer. Meanwhile, at the New England inn she runs, tight-assed French concierge Michel is disconsolate over the death of his obnoxious shihtzu dog. (The town is full of "characters.") Michel pushes Lorelai to help organize an elaborate funeral. It's an irritation amid her crisis, but she's dutiful. She recruits rock-musician friend Zack to play at the service, and the three go shopping for sheet music. It is a running gag that Michel is a Céline Dion fan (an inside joke, since the actor who plays him is from Montreal), so Michel insists, to Zack's agony, that the choice must be "My Heart Will Go On," his puppy's "favorite song."

At last the funeral arrives, in a room at the inn filled with flowers, Michel's friends and their own dogs. The camera pans past Zack, looking nice in a suit, playing a gentle classical-guitar arrangement of the song, to find Lorelai standing by the door. As the music continues—nylon strings rippling through this ode to a passion that spans all distances, up to and beyond the grave—Lorelai's face begins to quiver almost imperceptibly. A twilight falls behind her eyes. You can see she is realizing that her love for her husband is not as deep, not as true, as Michel's devotion to his awful pet. Or the tenderness Zack is bestowing on a tune he hates for Michel's sake. Or even the song's dreamy lyrics, which like Lorelai's feelings go unspoken but ring in our heads. She does not want Chris by her side unto death. That's the kind of love she wants to give, the kind he deserves, but she has to stop lying: it's not there. When she gets home, Chris asks how the funeral was. She just says, "Sad." And she sits him down to say how sorry she is, and goodbye.

My tears now are not only at the thought of having to abandon a love that's real, but wrong. Something has shifted. I'm no longer watching a show about a teenage girl, whether mother or daughter. It's become one about an adult, my age, admitting that to forge a decent happiness you can't keep trying to bend all the rules; you aren't exempt from the laws of motion that make the world turn. And one of the minor ones is that people need sentimental songs to marry, mourn and break up to, and this place they hold matters more than anything intrinsic to the songs themselves. In fact, when one of those weepy widescreen ballads lands just so, it can wise you up that you're just one more dumb dog that has to do its best to make things right until one day it dies. And that's sad. Sad enough to make you cry. Even to cry along with Céline Dion. So tonight I listened to her version once more, keeping that fictional funeral in mind. Something was gained in the subcultural translation: while my eyes didn't well over, neither were they completely dry.

When this album was first released I assumed that it was shallow, that it was beneath me. A decade later I don't see the advantage in holding yourself above things; down on the surface is where the action is, the first layer of the unfathomable depths. Down there is where your heart gets beaten up, but keeps on beating. It does go on and on. The story is true. It's a big thing, it's big Time, and then it's gone with the wind.

There's a Magnetic Fields song about "The Book of Love," the place, songwriter Stephin Merritt sings, "where music comes from." To sum up this new edition of Céline Dion's album, I can't improve on his conclusion: *Let's Talk About Love* "is long and boring / and written very long ago. / It's full of flowers and heart-shaped boxes / and things we're all too young to know."

12.
Let's Talk About Love

The virtuosity that cool audiences today applaud, the sort Céline always fumbles, is not about having a multioctave voice or flamenco-fast fingers: It's about being able to manipulate signs and symbols, to hitch them up and decouple them in a blink of an eye, to quote Homer but in the voice of Homer Simpson. It's the kind of virtuosity an advertiser deploys to hook multiple demographics, as well as the playful or caviling way of the postmodern artist. And while it is entirely a bravura performance of taste, it disavows having *a* taste, which would be boring, pathetic, embarrassing. In fact there's been something old-fashioned about this book, because "taste" is a word hardly anyone uses any more. We departed the twentieth century without any of the rationales for taste we came in with, so we circumvent the issue. While we play it as vigorously as ever, we make like we're on to taste's game. We pay it tribute by way of repression: We don't commend someone's *good taste* because we don't want to be caught wearing morning coats and waxed mustaches and asking what the devil is up with the wogs. We don't use *bad taste* except as a jocular antagonym in which bad means good. We say a song or a book or a movie is great or that it's shit, but admit nothing so stuffy or confining as having a system, a consistency to our freewheeling aesthetic target practice. We are omnivores. We devour everything. That way we never have to answer the question, "Who do you mean, 'we'?"

At the end of my immersion in Céline Dion, I can't claim to have learned what it's like to be a Céline fan, but I've been confronted with how much is involved in *not* being a Céline fan. Though I now enjoy some of her music, it's never in the same way I like "my" music, which tells me that I have a way of liking: it forces me to admit I have a taste. Yes, it was vain not to want the neighbors to hear me playing *Let's Talk About Love*. But the worst part was feeling ashamed to feel ashamed. Try it yourself: Pick some music you find particularly unattractive and crank it up every day for a couple of weeks. Or go out for the evening wearing clothes you find ugly, and not in a funny way. Before having a dinner date over, hang a painting from a Christian-art sale over your bed. (Really, do: reading about it is no substitute.) Shame has a way of throwing you back upon your own existence, on the unbearable truth that you are identical with you, that you are your limits. Which immediately makes the self feel incomplete, unjustified, a chasm of lack. It's the reverse of the sense of self-extension that having likes and dislikes usually provides. It is humbling.

A few people have asked me, isn't life too short to waste time on art you dislike? But lately I feel like life is too short *not* to. I began this experiment with an abstract question about how taste functions, but I've come to see that it was more personal: I am nearing my fortieth birthday, half-willingly being carried out the exit of youth culture, and I've begun to wonder what kind of person that will make me. I cringe when I think what a subcultural snob I was five or ten years ago, and worse in my teens and twenties, how vigilant I was against being *taken in*—unaware that I was also refusing an invitation *out*. In retrospect, this experiment seems like a last effort to purge that insularity, so that my next phase might happen in a larger world, one beyond the horizon of my habits. For me, adulthood is turning out to be about becoming democratic.

It wasn't why I chose her, but Céline turned out to be an apt figurehead for that expedition. She stinks of democracy, mingled with the odors of designer perfumes and of dollars, Euros and yen. Far more than most celebrities, she is plausible as a common person catapulted into uncommon status. Apart from her music, I've grown accustomed to her over-expressive face, attached to her arm-flinging gawkiness. And as I suspected, looking closely at her seemingly mundane music has focused me on another set of virtues—not so much the fidelity and devotion she sings about, but the persistence and flexibility it takes to translate between her terms and mine.

This is what I mean by democracy—not a limp open-mindedness, but actively grappling with people and things not like me, which brings with it the perilous question of what I am like. Democracy, that dangerous, paradoxical and mostly unattempted ideal, sees that the self *is* insufficient, dependent for definition on otherness, and chooses not only to accept that but to celebrate it, to stake everything on it. Through democracy, which demands we meet strangers as equals, we perhaps become less strangers to ourselves.

The historian and sociologist Richard Sennett, in books

such as *The Fall of Public Man*, argues that we can know ourselves fully only when we also know ourselves in public, and
western culture has become terribly bad at publicness. It's
not just that we lack shared spaces, and allow our resources,
culture, everything that contributes to the commonweal, to be
privatized rapaciously. It's the concept of human nature we've
adopted, which assumes that private life is more authentic
than public life: "We take it for granted," Sennett said in a
CBC Radio interview, "that when we are really present, when
we're really alive, really there for someone else, we're going
to be hidden from a crowd rather than in the midst of it."
He traces this viewpoint to the second half of the nineteenth
century, when the public cultures that had been evolving in
cosmopolitan cities went into retreat, due to elite paranoia
about crowds (mobs) and the rise of bourgeois family life and
psychology. Exteriors became suspect; the interior, inward-
ness, became the wellspring of truth. And that's the onramp
en route to the gated community.

It's not a coincidence, I think, that the late nineteenth
century also saw sentimentality villainized, cultural brow
levels more rigidly segregated, the poor kicked out of the
opera houses and Shakespeare banished from variety shows.
Preoccupations in art with authenticity, purity and depth
took firm hold. It all seems to relate to drawing a strong line
between private life and public interaction, refusing any relationship with art other than an intimate one. There's so much
cultural capital invested in the muscular aesthetic judgment:
we restrict our approval to what we can love, and sever ties
with any less certain constituencies.

Yet there are so many ways of loving music. You can love
a song for what you take to be its depth, formal elegance and

lasting value, the traditional parameters of purist art appreciation. But you can also love a song for its novelty, as a fresh
variation on the same old thing, in which case you may love
it only briefly (and later be fond of it in memorium of that
love, as a reminder of the pleasantness of having a past). The
critic Joshua Clover has argued that loving novelty is perfectly
appropriate, because the material conditions of mass culture
make it ever-renewable: if you wear out one pop song, there
will always be another. Ranking lastingness above novelty is
a holdover from an aesthetic of scarcity, predating the age of
mechanical, or digital, reproduction. So today we can love a
song for being one of many, part of the crowd, rather than
as an intimate partner. A rich taste life will include both, just
as a rich erotic life includes infatuations and flings as well
as long-term relationships, because they do different things
to us. (Don't we feel a bit sorry for people who marry their
high-school sweethearts, even as we admire their constancy?)
And luckily, songs are not jealous of one another, and don't
have any feelings to be hurt. They don't need our undivided
or permanent commitment.

You also can love a song for its datedness, for the social
history its anachronism reveals. You can love a song for how
its sentimentality gives a workout to the emotions. You can
love it for its foreignness, for the glimpse it gives of human
variability. You can love it for its exemplarity, for being the
"ultimate" disco floor filler or schmaltzy mother song. You
can love it for representing a place, a community, even an ideology, in the brokenhearted way I love "The Internationale."
You might love it for its popularity, for linking you to the
crowd: being popular may not make it "good" but it does
make it *a* good, and a service, and you can listen to learn what

it is doing for other people. As critic Ann Powers argued in her essay "Bread and Butter Songs," you might even love a song, like "Living on a Prayer" or "My Heart Will Go On," for its "meaningful unoriginality," for stirring up feelings in an everyday, readily absorbed way, rather than in a shock wave. Bread-and-butter songs are good for group yell-alongs.

You can only feel all these sorts of love if you're uncowed by the question of whether a song will stand the "test of time," which implies that to pass away, to die, is to fail (and that taste is about making predictions). You can't feel them if you're looking for the one record you would take to a desert island, a scenario designed to strip the conviviality from the aesthetic imagination. When all these varieties of love are allowed, taste can seem less like a bunch of high-school cliques or a global conspiracy of privilege and more like a fantasy world in which we get to romance or at least fool around with many strangers.

Love may be too strong a word. It sounds like *identification* and *empathy*. Sennett says that the moral value of public life depends instead on *sympathy*: To be able to say, "Your issues are not my issues, but I want to understand what they are. That, in my view," he told the CBC, "is a more respectful way for people to deal with cultural differences than, as it were, to *consume* them—to say, 'I'm putting on these ghetto duds, I'm going to talk like a black person, I'm really *with* them, y'know?' . . . Something that acknowledges both the effort to understand and social distance is a better way for people in complex communities to live. It actually allows you to have more relationship with them than if you pressure yourself to get as intimate and as close as possible . . . which is tyrannical: you tyrannize yourself and you tyrannize the other."

If I was trying to learn to love Céline Dion's music, then, perhaps my experiment was too tyrannical. It would be no solution to say we have to love everything, the equivalent of loving nothing. (As God does.) What counted in the end was to give *Let's Talk About Love* a sympathetic hearing, to credit that others find it lovable and ask what that can tell me about music (or globalism, or sentimentality) in general. The kind of contempt that's mobilized by "cool" taste is inimical to that sympathy, to an aesthetics that might support a good public life.

The goal is not that we all end up with the same taste, no matter how broad. That seems to be the tacit wish when someone claims to know a work's true value, or when Kant and Hegel suggest that under ideal conditions, we'd all reach aesthetic agreement. As philosopher Alexander Nehamas said in a 2001 lecture, this is an awful vision, out of *Invasion of the Body Snatchers*. To say everyone ought to like what I like is to suggest everyone should be alike. Taste, after all, is part of the character you present to others. Personality is a creative medium of its own. People depend on you to exhibit some consistency of taste, some sensibility, as they rely that you won't adopt diametrically opposed political views from one day to the next or keep switching in conversation into various foreign accents. So we ought to have musical loves and personal tastes, so long as we're not naive enough to think personal is all they are, or so selfish as to exclude other tastes from legitimacy.

That means somehow ratcheting down the Kantian mechanism that causes us, when we find something beautiful, to want everyone else to agree, and to consider them defective (satisfyingly, Bourdieu might add) if they don't. When we love a person, we don't want everyone else to feel the same way—it's bad enough if just one other person is in love with her. So instead of campaigning for our preferences to be generally adopted, we could try to relish the plenitude of tastes, to admire a well-put-together taste set that's alien to our own, the way I felt about Sophoan, the Cambodian-American Céline fan. I would be relieved to have fewer debates over who is right or wrong about music, and more that go, "Wow, you hate all the music I like and I hate everything you like. What might we make of that?"

What would criticism be like if it were not foremost trying to persuade people to find the same things great? If it weren't about making cases for or against things? It wouldn't need to adopt the kind of "objective" (or self-consciously hip) tone that conceals the identity and social location of the author, the better to win you over. It might be more frank about the two-sidedness of aesthetic encounter, and offer something more like a tour of an aesthetic experience, a travelogue, a memoir. More and more critics, in fact, are incorporating personal narrative into their work. Perhaps this is the benefit of the explosion of cultural judgment on the Internet, where millions of thumbs turn up and down daily: by rendering their traditional job of arbitration obsolete, it frees critics to find other ways of contemplating music.

Bourdieu, for one, thought criticism should concern itself with context, with locating artists and their audiences socially, trying to outline for whom, to whom and by what channels an artwork speaks. As usual, he went too far, claiming this was the only morally defensible kind of criticism. But we could use much more of it. Besides travelogue and memoir, criticism could become like a detective story.

As well, in swearing off Kantian disinterest, the critic could become a more openly *interested, invested* observer. We could provide accounts of all we expect out of music, all the things music accomplishes when it is, as musicologist Christopher Small puts it, "musicking." In daily life music is usually part of other activities, from dancing to housework to sex to gossip to dinner. In critical discourse it's as if the only action going on when music is playing is the activity of evaluating music. The question becomes, "Is this good music to listen to while you're making aesthetic judgments?" Which may explain what makes some bands critics' darlings: Sonic Youth, for instance, is not great music to dance to, but it's a terrific soundtrack for making aesthetic judgments. (Part of the reason for the recent backlash against indie rock, I suspect, is a weariness with how much of it seems to be mainly music to judge music by.) Céline Dion, on the other hand, is lousy music to make aesthetic judgments to, but might be excellent for having a first kiss, or burying your grandma, or breaking down in tears.

You can't go on suspending judgment forever—that would be to forgo genuinely enjoying music, since you can't enjoy what you can't like. But a more pluralistic criticism might put less stock in defending its choices and more in depicting its enjoyment, with all its messiness and private soul tremors—to show what it is *like* for me to like it, and invite you to compare. This kind of exchange takes place sometimes between critics on the Internet, and it would be fascinating to have more dialogic criticism: here is my story, what is yours? You might have to be ready, like Céline, to be laughed at. (Judge not, as the Bible sort of says, unless you're eager to be judged.) In these ways the embarrassment of having a taste, the reflexive disgust of distinction, the strangeness of our strangeness to one another, might get the airing they need. As Marx once wrote, "Shame is a revolutionary sentiment." Obviously, reforming the way we talk about music is on its own no way to fix social injustice or the degradation of public life—but if we're going to be talking anyway, we could at least stop making matters worse.

All that said, failed art and (one hopes) great art do exist, and it is worth continuing to talk about which is which, however compromised the conversation might be. It is probably totally subjective whether you prefer Céline Dion or the White Stripes, and a case of social prejudice that Céline is less cool than that band's Jack White. But it seems fair to guess neither of them can rival the Beatles or Louis Armstrong—based, for example, on how broadly (one might say democratically) those artists appeal to people across taste divides. When we do make judgments, though, the trick would be to remember that they are contingent, hailing from one small point in time and in society. It's only a rough draft of art history: it always could be otherwise, and usually will be. The thrill is that as a rough draft, it is always up for revision, so we are constantly at risk of our minds being changed—the promise that lured us all to art in the first place.

How will art itself deal with having journeyed beyond the end of taste, with—as "America's Most Wanted" painter Alex Melamid said—artists' status as "the minority that *knows*" having given way to a period when they are as shaky and unsure of how to use their taste as anyone else living in a complex community? If taste is largely a tangle of social relationships, can art find means of untangling them? It's hard to guess. It surely won't be with art that sits in judgment of its audience. Perhaps it would be an art of translation. Some artists are taking the social itself as their medium, as Komar and Melamid did in their poll-based paintings, and others have done with "relational aesthetics" that make art out of a party or a game, and still others by trading call-and-response creativity on networks such as YouTube. They come from many levels of shame and shamelessness, but they have in common that they all hazard to collaborate with strangers. Some of this stuff is tough even to recognize as art, but after a period when art often seemed to be its own main subject, it's refreshing to have art in which its newness consists in letting in the world, even too much of it. Maybe there will be more variety shows.

* * *

Meanwhile, Céline has been changing too. She seems to have come into her own as an adult, to have made a much-belated discovery that she has a self, ever since her husband's battle with cancer and the birth of their son René Charles (who, according to press reports, is totally into hard rock music). Her four-year run of *A New Day* in Las Vegas, meanwhile, has worn down the skeptics and helped make Vegas an established music center. The windup at the end of 2007 will no doubt be triumphant.

But the evolution is also in her music. Céline's albums since *Let's Talk About Love* have gained some restraint, the singing and arrangements become more up-to-date and "tasteful." Her latest French release, *D'Elles*, goes very high-culture, even intellectual—it's a concept album in which all the lyrics were provided by female journalists and novelists from Quebec and France. (One review was titled, "I Am Woman, Hear Me Think.") At the 2007 Oscars, she was asked to sing a new piece by the renowned (and cosmopolitanly hip) Italian film composer Ennio Morricone, who was receiving a lifetime-achievement award. And her next album might go even further. Titled, warningly to fans, *Taking Chances*, it is rumored at the time of this writing to include songs by the rock band Evanescence, ex-Eurythmics musician Dave Stewart, the R&B artists Ne-Yo and R. Kelly (who's built up cachet with the loony audacity of his musical soap opera, "Trapped in the Closet"), producer The-Dream (who made Rihanna's massive hit "Umbrella") and, most unlikely of all, that chart-topping studio avant-gardist, Timbaland. It is almost as if Céline has figured out how to be cool, American-style.

Meanwhile in the summer of 2007 in Toronto and Montreal, two separate fringe-theater plays featuring Céline impersonators popped up, one a satire based on her life called *Céline Speaks* and the other a drag-queen murder mystery called *Saving Céline*. And *Elle* magazine called me for comment for an article that questioned if Céline is as uncool as everybody thinks. Maybe Simon Frith was wrong: maybe Céline *is* a candidate for critical redemption. Camp treatments and revisionist articles are surely portents.

In both Bourdieuvian and show-business terms, this was all predictable: having been at the summit of the entertainment field for so long, Céline was bound to begin finding ways of converting her quickly devaluing 90s cultural capital into a more liquid currency, and teaming with cool producers has become a standard move for performers in mid-career or later who need a shot of credibility. Don't be surprised if in a decade she is working with Rick Rubin, who did the trick for Johnny Cash and Neil Diamond, or Jack White, who gave a boost to Loretta Lynn. Perhaps those lost Phil Spector tapes will leak out of the vaults.

All of which, I confess, makes me slightly sad. It looks like a narrowing of options: if even Céline has finally gotten sucked into the widening gyre of competitive distinction that is cool, how much hope is there that any of us can resist its slick blandishments?

I'm reassured, however, by the biggest Céline-related news of the year, which was that in an ostensibly *American Idol*-style contest on the Internet, her song "You and I" was selected as Democratic candidate Hillary Clinton's campaign song for the 2008 presidential primaries. As the Platonic form of the *Idol* talent-contest winner, of course, Céline had been a shoo-in. And to court such potential voters as older women of all income brackets, suburban families, new immigrants and more, she was probably a savvy choice: indeed, for once, Hillary Clinton seemed to have managed a solidly populist move, to help palliate her aura of graspingness and self-regard.

And what happened? Of course, the announcement was met with moans, groans and rampant smart-aleckery from music blogs, late-night talk shows and Sunday newspaper columns.

So far, it seems, Céline Dion remains securely uncool. And that gives me the heart to go on.

Acknowledgments

Along with the cited authors, this book owes much, for time and generosity as interview subjects, information suppliers or idea stimulators, to Jody Rosen, Frank Kogan, Simon Frith, Line Grenier, Kathy Meizel, Jason Gross, Simon Reynolds, John Shaw, Jake London, Eric Weisbard, Ann Powers, Candice Rainey (*Elle* magazine), Garnette Cadogan, David Cantwell, Barry Mazor, Dan Bejar, Stephanie Verge, Joe Nielsen, Sophoan Sorn, Gwen Ansell, Kim Jakwerth, Alex Serpa, Itmar BZ, Elaine Trevizan de Souza, Parul Pandya, Angela Hiler, Nina Melechen, JD Considine, Sean Michaels, Michelangelo Matos, Matt Perpetua, Douglas Wolk, Brian Joseph Davis, Brian Mansfield, Martha Hume, Carl A. Zimring, Jon Weisberger, Ron Warnick, Erella Ganon, Mike Powell, Michael Barthel, Ari Abramowitz, Mani Haghighi, Matt Collins, Patrick Roscoe and Ker Wells. For past conversations on these themes, thank you to Heather Mackay, Buffy Childerhose, Doug Saunders, Katerina Cizek, Dana

Truby and Scott Straus. For patience above and beyond, thanks to 33 1/3 editor David Barker, and my colleagues at *The Globe and Mail* in Toronto. For ears and fuel, thanks to the EMP Pop Conference and all who attend. Kate McGee, Laurie McGregor and Chris Randle provided invaluable and poorly paid research assistance.

For help, feedback and life sustenance, unspeakable thanks to Misha Glouberman, Julia Rosenberg, Eric Smith, Susana Bejar, Katarina Gligorijevic Collins, Sean Dixon, Lauren Bride, Ryan Kamstra, Michael McManus, Katie Krelove and Colette Wilson.

Margaux Williamson was my comrade-in-arms.

And this book is for Sheila Heti, with what else but love.

More praise for the 33 1/3 series:

We . . . aren't naive enough to think that we're your only source for reading about music (but if we had our way . . . watch out). For those of you who really like to know everything there is to know about an album, you'd do well to check out Continuum's "33 1/3" series of books.—*Pitchfork*

As individualistic and idiosyncratic as the albums that inspired them—Rob Trucks, *Cleveland Scene*

The best albums ever made—turned into books!—*Blender* magazine

This is some of the best music writing going on right now—*Pulse of the Twin Cities*

Music writing done right—*Tape Op* magazine

Admirable. . . . 33 1/3 has broken new ground—*THES* (UK)

The series quietly breathes some life into the world of music fanaticism . . . an explosion of sincere, humbled appreciation—*The Portland Mercury*

The series represents the Holy Grail of millions of late Baby Boomers—*All About Jazz*

Inspired—*Details*

Neat—Nick Hornby, *The Believer*

A much-needed reprieve from the bite-size capsule reviews that rule much of today's music criticism—*San Francisco Bay Guardian*

Informed, fun and personal—*Paste Magazine*

The series tries to inject new life into a tired form—*Newsday*

All [these] books revel in the distinct shapes and benefits of an album, its ability to go places film, prose or sculpture can't reach, while capable of being as awe-inspiring as the best of those mediums—*Philadelphia City Paper*

These first few installments set the bar pretty high for those to come—*Tangents*

At their best, these Continuum books make rich, thought-provoking arguments for the song collections at hand—*The Philadelphia Inquirer*

A really remarkable new series of books—*The Sunday News-Herald, Michigan*

A brilliant idea—*The Times* (London)

The series treats its subjects with the kind of intelligence and carefully considered respect they deserve—*Pop Culture Press*

Lucid . . . each volume provides insightful commentary—*The Paper, Central Illinois*

Idiosyncratic, pocket-sized monographs done with passion and insight . . . the analysis is both personal and articulate—*Harp Magazine*

The series delves as deep as it's possible to go without resorting to padding . . . 5 stars each—*Classic Rock Magazine* (UK)

Passionate, astutely written, and they lend real insight—*Amplifier Magazine*

If an enterprising college professor were to put together a course on pop criticism and classic rock 'n' roll records, the textbooks could clearly be found among the . . . 33 1/3 series presented by Continuum Books. Each book delves deeply into an iconic album of the past 40 years, with a variety of approaches—*St. Louis Post-Dispatch*

Informative, thought-provoking, creative, obsessive and more—*Albany Times Union*

Articulate, well-researched, and passionate—*Library Journal*

A cracking good idea, and if you like the albums in question, you're sure to love the books—*Leaf Salon,* New Zealand

Eclectic enough that there should be something for everyone—*Maxim*

A nifty little string of books that deserves more attention—*Columbia Daily Tribune*

These little tomes have captured me in a gobsmacked haze. . . . These writings are so vivid and uplifting—*Cincinnati City Beat*

Cultural elitism never had it so good—*Louisville Eccentric Observer*

Praise for individual titles in the series:

<u>Meat Is Murder</u>

My personal favorite of the batch has to be Joe Pernice's autobiographic-fiction fantasia. . . . Over little more than a hundred pages, he manages a vivid recollection of a teenage New England Catholic school life circa 1985, in all its conflict and alienation, sexual fumblings and misplaced longing—*Tangents*

Pernice's novella captures these feelings of the despair of possibility, of rushing out to meet the world and the world rushing in to meet you, and the price of that meeting. As sound-tracked by the Smiths—*Drowned in Sound*

Pernice hits his mark. The well-developed sense of character, plot and pacing shows that he has serious promise as a novelist. His emotionally precise imagery can be bluntly, chillingly personal—*The Boston Weekly Dig*

Continuum . . . knew what they were doing when they asked songwriter Joe Pernice to pay homage to the Smiths' *Meat Is Murder*—*Austin American-Statesman*

Pernice's writing style reminded me of Douglas Coupland's: the embodiment of youthful vitality and innocent cynicism, clever, quick-witted, and aware of the ridiculous cultural symbols of his time—*Stylus Magazine* (University of Winnipeg)

Forever Changes

Love fan Andrew Hultkrans obsesses brilliantly on the rock legends' seminal disc—*Vanity Fair*

Dusty in Memphis

Warren is a greatly gifted good heart, and I love him. Read his book, listen to his record, and you will too—Stanley Booth, author of *The True Adventures of the Rolling Stones*

Warren Zanes . . . is so in love with Dusty Springfield's great 1969 adventure in tortured Dixie soul that he's willing to jump off the deep end in writing about it. Artfully blending academic citation, personal memoir and pungent commentary from *Dusty in Memphis* principals such as producer Jerry Wexler, Zanes uses the record as a springboard into the myths and true mysteries of Southern life—*Rolling Stone* (4 star review)

James Brown Live at the Apollo

Masterful—*The Big Takeover*

Exemplary. . . . Most astonishing, however, is Wolk's conjecture that to avoid recording distortion, the riotous album captured "James Brown holding back"—*Mojo* (UK)

Let It Be (Replacements)

These are solid short-short stories with bona fide epiphanies—that they shed light on Meloy's past only makes them more engaging—*Village Voice*

For reviews of individual titles in the series, please visit our web-site at www.continuumbooks.com and 33third.blogspot.com